Joy Comes with the Mourning

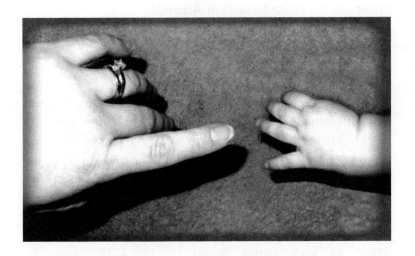

The miracles of my miscarriages and other testimonies of
God's grace, peace, and joy, after the loss of a child.

Holly M. Besser

In Memory of:

Our unborn blessings – never in our arms,
but always in our hearts.

Dedicated to:

The children God will place into our arms as well as our hearts, and also to Dr. Carol Miller, without whom none of this would be possible.

Thank You to:

All who made this book possible: First of all, to God, who placed this idea in my heart, and gave me the patience and endurance to see it through. Secondly, to Kevin, my wonderful husband, who spent countless hours reading and re-reading my manuscript over the past year and a half. He is an amazing father to our children, and a constant support as my best friend. Last, but certainly not least, thank you to all those who participated in writing testimonies in this book. I pray that God will bless you richly for following Him in the obedience of sharing your joy and healing, in the midst of pain and grief, in an effort to minister to others.

Table of Contents

A baby's milestones during pregnancy

Day 1: Approximately 200,000,000 sperm try to pass through into Mom's egg. Only one succeeds. All of this new baby's features, such as sex, eye color, hair color, etc., are already decided by 46 chromosomes — half received from Mom and half from Dad.

Day 21: The heart begins to beat.

By the end of Month 1: 1/8 inch (about the size of the tip of a pen) and way under 1 ounce
- The arms and legs appear as tiny buds.
- The mouth and nose begin to take shape.
- The eyes begin to develop and the ears can now be seen.
- Brain and spinal cord start to grow.
- Lungs start to develop.

Day 44: 99% of the muscles are developed.

By the end of Month 2: 1 inch (about the size of a thumb) and about 1/4 ounce
- Fingers and toes begin to form.
- The inner ear and the eyelids begin to develop.
- Bones can be seen.
- All major organs and systems are present.

Week 12: The baby can swallow and respond to stimulation.

By the end of Month 3: 3 inches and about 1 ounce
- Fingernails and toenails start to form.
- Intestines begin growing.
- Tiny buds appear for twenty future teeth.
- Fingerprints are clear and unique.

By the end of Month 4: 5 inches and nearly 5 ounces
- Sex organs are formed.
- The outer ear begins to develop and the baby can now hear.
- Kidneys are working and can produce urine.
- Arms and legs can move. Hands can grip.
- Somersaults!

By the end of Month 5: 10 inches and ½ - 1 pound
- Eyebrows and eyelashes can be seen.
- Baby can suck his/her thumb.
- Fingernails are completely developed.
- The mom can likely begin to feel movements now.

By the end of Month 6: 12 inches and about 1 ½ pounds
- Hair begins to grow.
- Eyes begin to open.
- Lungs are fully formed, but not working yet.
- The brain begins to develop much more rapidly.

By the end of Month 7: 15 inches and nearly 3 pounds
- Eyes can follow light, and can open and close.
- The baby can kick and stretch.
- The baby responds to sounds outside the womb.

By the end of Month 8: 18 inches and almost 5 pounds
- Bones grow harder.
- Brain is developing different regions.
- The baby's tongue has taste buds, and can taste sweet and sour.
- The baby can hiccup.
- Gaining weight fast.

By the end of Month 9: around 20 inches and average of 6-9 pounds
- Turns head-down for birth.
- Skin smoothes out.
- Lungs are ready to work.
- Baby gains ½ pound per week.

Forward

Growing up as the youngest child in my family, I never had the opportunity to witness my mother pregnant or to experience other such things that accompany a younger sibling's birth. My introduction to understanding and to just being around babies and young children truly came after my wife and I were married. We began our church ministry together by volunteering in our church nursery. Holly and I had always talked about having children, even back when we were first dating. She was a junior in high school, and I was a college freshman. My wife had *always* wanted to be a mother, ever since she was quite young. By the time we were married in 2000, this desire had grown into a remarkably strong longing.

I believe that a desire for children is a great aspiration that the Lord gives to most women; however, it seemed that my wife had received an extra helping of this God-given gift. Men, on the other hand, are often said to be the exact opposite. Many times we are referred to as having either very little enthusiasm towards children or of being just plain indifferent towards them. Both of these described me. As a young man, I always wanted to have children and to be a father, but the idea of it actually being a reality and the emotions connected with it definitely did not come, until I experienced parenthood for myself.

During the first several years of our marriage, the likelihood of having children was in question. Then, at the beginning of 2008, the Lord blessed us with our first son. Witnessing the miracle of the pregnancy and birth of Channing was, not only life-changing, but also heart-changing for me. Going through the struggles and events, leading up to, during, and after the birth of Channing was an amazing experience. Even though it was not easy, looking back now, I can certainly see how all of the circumstances, surrounding this blessing, worked together to strengthened our relationship with each other and with Christ.

I can remember well the conversations that led to the future expansion of our family. I was excited and looking forward to what the Lord would have in store for us, should He choose to bless us with another child. Honestly, I had never given miscarriage a thought, until it actually happened. The look on Holly's face, in the ultrasound room that day, and then, later, tearfully texting my parents the news that our baby had no heartbeat, are two things that I will never forget.

Holly has been amazingly strong throughout her pregnancies, with each of our children. She feels blessed to have had the opportunity to carry each one of our five children – our two boys, who are continual blessings in our home each day, and also, the three God chose to take to heaven, before birth, for His glory. God has given my wife a strong passion and a true empathy for women, who have experienced the loss of a child. In our society, grieving the death of an unborn child is often treated as taboo and, in some cases, is considered unnecessary and even ridiculous. Even in Christian circles, mourning a miscarriage is frequently misconstrued as being "unspiritual" or lacking in faith. During the course of writing this book, Holly has worked through her grief, studied scripture, and spoken with so many other hurting women (many of whom have been hurting for decades). Through her faithful effort, I have seen how God's plan always works out for our good and for His glory in each of our lives.

The circumstances, burdens, and trials of life, while many times are difficult and frequently seem impossible to bear, are intended for a purpose. I hope that, as you read my wife's story and the stories of the many other women, included in this book, you will see evidence that Jesus Christ loves us unconditionally, and that He desires a relationship with us. I pray that you will find reassurance that in all of the situations in our lives, whether they are big or small, simple or complex, straight-forward or unimaginable, He promises to grant a peace that passes all understanding. May we seek to be a testimony to those around us, that they may see a reflection of Christ is us, as we exhibit the eternal joy that comes with the mourning.

- Kevin M. Besser

Introduction

M y goal in this book is to lay the groundwork for understanding the many emotions that accompany the loss of a child. Not only are there emotions for the parents to deal with, but also for family members, friends, and acquaintances of those experiencing this loss. I desire to help those who have not suffered the death of a child, to better understand and sympathize with those who *have* been touched by this significant loss in their life. For those who may someday experience this terrible heartbreak, I hope the testimonies, which follow each chapter, may help prepare you to handle the emotional strain that such a loss brings. Most of all, I want to empathize with those of you who have already felt the grief associated with losing a child, in the hope that you will find, not only peace and comfort, but also the courage to share *your* story with those around you. Without doubt, sharing with others is extremely helpful in the healing process, but it is also a miraculous opportunity to testify to God's amazing grace.

Romans 5:2 - By whom also we have access by faith into this grace wherein we stand, and rejoice in hope of the glory of God.

The purpose of this book is perhaps a bit different than most books you may have read on this subject. My objective is not to tell you how you could, would, or should be feeling after the loss of a child. Neither do I want to try to make you hurt or heal in the same manner as I have. My desire and my hope is that I might encourage and remind you that you are not alone, that what you are feeling is real and legitimate, and that God has a plan to bring grace, peace and even joy through this significant loss in your life.

I pray that you will not allow anything that I say to become a stumbling block to you, but rather, you will realize that we all deal with trials in our lives in different and unique ways. I hope you will find healing for your heart and soul within the arms of the almighty and loving Heavenly Father. I also desire that, no matter what stage of this process you currently find yourself in, you will discover ways to bless and touch those around you with hope.

> **II Corinthians 1:4** - *Who comforteth us in all our tribulation, that we may be able to comfort them which are in any trouble, by the comfort wherewith we ourselves are comforted of God.*

May God grant you an open heart and mind as you share in this small, yet very personal, part of my life and the lives of those who have shared in this book. God bless you as you seek to experience the "joy that comes with the mourning."

Psalm 30
A Psalm of David.

1 I will extol you, O LORD, for you have drawn me up
and have not let my foes rejoice over me.
2 O LORD my God, I cried to you for help,
and you have healed me.
3 O LORD, you have brought up my soul from Sheol;
you restored me to life from among those
who go down to the pit.
4 Sing praises to the LORD, O you his saints,
and give thanks to his holy name.
5 For his anger is but for a moment,
and his favor is for a lifetime.
Weeping may tarry for the night,
but joy comes with the morning.
6 As for me, I said in my prosperity,
"I shall never be moved."
7 By your favor, O LORD,
you made my mountain stand strong;
you hid your face; I was dismayed.
8 To you, O LORD, I cry,
and to the Lord I plead for mercy:
9 "What profit is there in my death,
if I go down to the pit?
Will the dust praise you?
Will it tell of your faithfulness?
10 Hear, O LORD, and be merciful to me!
O LORD, be my helper!"
11 You have turned for me my mourning into dancing;
you have loosed my sackcloth
and clothed me with gladness,
12 that my glory may sing your praise and not be silent.
O LORD my God, I will give thanks to you forever!

-❧ Chapter 1 ❧-

The Miracle of Desire

I never had any intention of writing a book of any kind. I have always enjoyed writing, but I certainly would never consider myself to be an "author" - not by any stretch of the imagination. However, God had a different plan. So, let me begin this "calling" by telling you just a little about what has brought me to this place in my life. I was raised in a Protestant, Christian home by both of my parents. I have two younger sisters and a younger brother. I am thirteen years older than my youngest sister, so I was more like a second "mommy" than an older sister. I spent a lot of time with my siblings – taking care of them and playing with them. My Mother let me be very "hands-on," which allowed me to discover a special place in my heart for children. When I was fifteen, I began working for a Christian daycare at the school I attended. I learned a lot about the legalities of childcare, which taught me the importance of thinking about the "what ifs" in life. After finishing school, I worked for several other daycare centers and also as a nanny, to two different families. I had a few other jobs, but I knew that caring for children was definitely my one and only career goal. I wanted to be a full-time Mommy!

My husband, Kevin, and I were married in August of 2000. We had started dating right before my sixteenth birthday, so we did not have many "surprises" to deal with after the wedding. We were (and still are) best friends. We had just enough in common to enjoy each other's constant company, and just enough differences to find each other interesting. We were (and still are) a "match made in heaven." We had often discussed our ideas for our future and a family. We knew that children were definitely a gift from God, which we desired to experience first-hand. We decided to wait a few years, and spend some time together doing things that we would have a hard time doing with children, such as traveling and building our first home.

In February of 2002, I began a very low-key exercise routine to try to get into shape. After about two weeks, I began to experience some lower back pain. I figured that it had something to do with my job – which, at the time, involved a lot of sitting. I didn't worry about it too much, until a couple of weeks later, when it became constant. I decided to go to a local physicians' assistant to get something to help with the pain. She recommended prescription non-aspirin, and sent me home. After a week or so, the pain didn't subside, so I went back to see her. She decided to try an oral steroid to test the severity of the problem. When the entire regiment of steroids did nothing to stop the pain, she sent me for x-rays and then, to an orthopedic specialist. By this point, I was pretty nervous. I had never had any health issues, besides some thyroid problems, and didn't really know what to expect. After having the required x-rays for insurance's sake, MRIs were ordered. My life was about to change in ways that I could never have imagined.

Proverbs 16:9 - A man's heart deviseth his way: but the LORD directeth his steps.

This was the beginning of several years of specialist, surgeons, and medications. Unfortunately, the answers that I got were very few and far between. I was told by one doctor that my back was degenerative to the extent that a 65 year old's back might be. I was given a suggested diagnosis of Degenerative Disc Disease "with complications." It was the elusive "complications" that were causing the problems, but no one seemed to know what "they" were. I was given many suggestions for a future diagnoses from "You should be just fine." to "You might need a wheelchair by 40, who can tell?" I was sent for nearly every treatment possible: chiropractic, spinal decompression therapy, physical therapy, and injections. I even explored ways to correct my posture and the way that I walk, by using a lift in my shoe, which elevated my slightly-shorter leg. It was suggested several times that I try water therapy, acupuncture, and even meditation. However, I felt that I had to draw the line somewhere. It could quickly take over my life, and this was certainly not the path that I had pictured my life taking.

> *Isaiah 55:8, 9* - *For my thoughts are not your thoughts, neither are your ways my ways, saith the LORD. For as the heavens are higher than the earth, so are my ways higher than your ways, and my thoughts than your thoughts.*

Over the course of several years, the only thing that all 20+ doctors/specialists seemed to agree on was the fact that my spine may not be able to support the weight associated with a pregnancy. Eventually, they also agreed that, because nothing else was working, I would need to resort to a regular regiment of narcotics and muscle-relaxers to allow me to live a somewhat-normal life.

By December of 2002, the pain had increased to the point that I could no longer walk without severe spasms and unbelievable pain shooting throughout my whole body 24 hours a day. I hated the thought of being dependent on pain-killers, especially when they did not "cure" me, but I had to choose a quality of life for myself...and my husband. Lying in bed all day just was not a valid or attractive option for me – not even during a pregnancy, which I wanted so badly.

As the years went by, we tried to wait patiently. We were not entirely sure what we were waiting for, but we continued to wait, anyhow. We truly believed that God wanted us to be parents, but we could not see the way in which He would make this possible. Looking back, I truly believe that God was using this time to prepare us for what He had planned.

Psalm 10:17 - LORD, thou hast heard the desire of the humble: thou wilt prepare their heart, thou wilt cause thine ear to hear.

We had discussed adoption, but even though I felt that I had surrendered this area to God and was willing to go this route, Kevin was just not quite ready to give up the dream of having biological children. So, we decided to give it another year and just keep trusting God to lead us. If after the year was up, we could not get any closer to figuring out a solution to my health issues, we would look into beginning the long process of adoption.

James 1:3-4 - Knowing this, that the trying of your faith worketh patience. But let patience have her perfect work, that ye may be perfect and entire, wanting nothing.

It was May of 2007, and I had an appointment to see my OBGYN. I rarely saw her, as she was usually booked out for months in advance. Usually, my appointments were with a physicians' assistant, as they were just routine check-ups. For a reason, which God ordained and orchestrated, the secretary "mistakenly" scheduled this appointment with the doctor. Dr. Carol Miller, my OBGYN, is an amazing woman. She is a godly and kind person, with enough loving compassion for everyone. I am always blessed by her gentle touch and sweet words. I had no plans for discussing pregnancy at this appointment; otherwise, I would have brought Kevin along. He had been beside me every single step on the crazy path that my health had taken me. However, when I realized that I was actually going to see Dr. Miller for the first time since my spine issues began, I started to formulate questions in my mind. I did not want to seem silly or reckless, especially after hearing 20+ opinions, over the past five years – all with the same conclusion: "Do not get pregnant." However, I just felt I could not see her without at least asking once more. I really admired Dr. Miller and I knew that her answer would cement the decision in my mind once and for all.

To my surprise, my doctor felt nearly 100% confident that my body would metabolize the narcotics and that the pregnancy would be completely safe. She also felt relatively sure that she could monitor my pain closely enough in order to avoid a great deal of further damage to or stress on my degenerative discs. She encouraged me to research it and to pray about it with Kevin. We spent several days researching and praying, but we felt that just receiving a positive answer from a physician was almost like hearing God speak to us directly. We were finally going to have a baby, and start our family! Well, to make a short story even shorter, let's just say that I was pregnant within the week. I had been taken off the pill, over a year before, due to high blood pressure, so we did not have any problems with that interfering. It had all happened so fast! God had chosen the exact timing of this long-awaited miracle, and we had finally "stumbled" upon it!

Ecclesiastes 3:11- *He hath made every thing beautiful in his time...*

We had our son, Channing Mark, in January of 2008, after thirteen hours of induced, natural childbirth. Now,

before you get the wrong impression, I begged for an epidural by the tenth hour, but they refused, without knowing
the complete history of my back issues. I determined, then
and there, that I would *never* be induced without an epidural
again! (I will fill you in on the details in a later chapter.)
Anyhow, our son was born completely healthy, and so hand-
some! We wouldn't have changed a thing about him. Even
the attending pediatrician told us that rarely is a child born
without even a hint of an imperfection, but he was perfect in
every way. He did not have any effects from the narcotics,
which all the doctors were so concerned about. God had not
only given us the desire for a family, but He had also made
a way for us to have one as well. Once God calls us to do
something, He always enables us to do it – in *His* time.

> *Psalm 18:32 - It is God that girdeth me with strength,
> and maketh my way perfect.*

During the years before Channing was born, I learned
several things about this amazing emotion called "desire."
I believe that there are two major types inside each of us:
"God-given" desires and "self-driven" desires. I had always
possessed the "God-given" desire for children my entire life
- from the time I babysat my siblings until the day my own
child was born. Some women are given more than others
and some, maybe, none at all. As for the "self-driven" desire,
this is as diverse as the individual and can change with time
and circumstance. I don't believe that any of us has the same
exact circumstances or the same exact personality that come
together to form this "self-driven" desire. In my case, waiting
for many years in complete uncertainty, escalated this desire
significantly. Often, it seems that the harder we have to work
towards a desired goal, the more we will desire it, and ultimately, appreciate it, if and when we achieve or receive it.
However, I also had to learn that I needed to entrust God with

the desires I had, and that I should concentrate on finding my contentment in Him alone. I could not choose to follow one part of God's commands and ignore the parts that I did not especially like or "feel" like doing. This was certainly far from being an easy task.

> ***Psalm 37:4-5*** - *Delight thyself also in the LORD: and he shall give thee the desires of thine heart. Commit thy way unto the LORD; trust also in him; and he shall bring it to pass.*

On the same note, our experiences are working to help shape our response to circumstances around us. I found that I tended to be more protective of my child, than many other parents around me. I was even a bit fearful at times. I traced this back to when Channing came down with a severe cold at 5 weeks old, and my whole idea about "germs" changed. I no longer wanted him on the nursery floor at church, or around another child with the "sniffles." My view of my responsibility as a mother was "filtered" by what I had experienced. In reality, I have learned that my child's safety is not, and never was, the dilemma. The condition of my walk with God is, and always was, the true issue. I need to trust Him with this child that He has loaned to me.

> ***Psalm 127:3*** - *Lo, children are an heritage of the LORD: and the fruit of the womb is his reward.*

> ***Proverbs 22:6*** - *Train up a child in the way he should go: and when he is old, he will not depart from it.*

I have also learned that this experience can certainly make me much more understanding and tolerant to other mother's seemingly over-protective desires and feelings.

Putting myself into someone else's shoes becomes that much easier.

Proverbs 31:26 - *She openeth her mouth with wisdom; and in her tongue is the law of kindness.*

On the other hand, I have seen the exact opposite be true as well. I have seen women, especially those with very little "God-given" *or* "self-driven" desire to parent, have the ability to "pop" babies out with such ease. It often seems that they have near-apathy towards their children. Some spend more time complaining about their children, than they actually do taking care of them. It seems they are always looking for the next opportunity to "dump" the kids on grandma and grandpa or even on their husbands, so they can have some more "me-time." I have had such trouble holding my tongue in conversations with these moms. Sometimes, I have had all I could do to keep from telling them exactly how I felt about them and their flawed thinking.

In the same way, my anger burns when I see a pregnant woman smoking or drinking. How dare she take such a chance with that little life growing inside of her? She chose to get pregnant, for goodness-sakes, she should accept the consequences associated with that decision! "Angry" hardly begins to describe how I feel about a woman's "right to choose." Not only does this seem like a terrible oxymoron, but it also seems so ridiculous. What choice do the women like me have – those of us who *want* to keep their babies, but they die anyway? No one asked me if I wanted a miscarriage. How dare someone even assume that their unborn child will live through the pregnancy to enter this world? Each life is so very precious. Truly, God is the only one with the right to "choose" the length of each life.

Job 33:4 - The spirit of God hath made me, and the breath of the Almighty hath given me life.

Job 14:5 - Seeing his days are determined, the number of his months are with thee, thou hast appointed his bounds that he cannot pass.

Even though I think that my anger was and is justified and righteous, the comparisons that I was making were destroying any contentment that I could have found in God. I think that sometimes we find it easier to lash out at everyone possible in the hopes of maybe "hitting" the person responsible for our pain.

While I was busy judging those around me, I had a problem of my own, which was getting out of control. It was definitely not obvious to everyone around me, but I was dealing with a bad case of post-partum depression, mixed with a selfish fear of losing my "identity." As for the post-partum, that was easily solved after filling out a short survey at the doctor's office, nine months after my son's birth. My only regret was that I waited so long to get help. Honestly, I had thought that I was sinning, and that I really just needed to pray more, or get my heart more focused on God. I feel that I wasted some of the best months of my son's life, living in an awful haze of frustration and discouragement. Most of all, I missed out on the joys of holding him at night, while I fed him. Night-time was the worst. I found that when you are in the middle of the depression, it is really hard to sort it out and ask for help. I am so very thankful for our family doctor, who did not judge me or condemn me, but quickly made arrangements to help me.

It took a bit longer to deal with the selfishness in my heart. It was not until I had hit the end of my proverbial "rope," and drove my husband into silence, that I was ready to come to God with my problem. Literally, within days, He showed me that my identity did not lie within myself, but in what I was created to do. The following passage describes this Biblical calling:

Proverbs 31:10-31 - *Who can find a virtuous woman? for her price is far above rubies. The heart of her husband doth safely trust in her, so that he shall have no need of spoil. She will do him good and not evil all the days of her life. She seeketh wool, and flax, and worketh willingly with her hands. She is like the merchants' ships; she bringeth her food from afar. She riseth also while it is yet night, and giveth meat to her household, and a portion to her maidens. She considereth a field, and buyeth it: with the fruit of her hands she planteth a vineyard. She girdeth her loins with strength, and strengtheneth her arms. She perceiveth that her merchandise is good: her candle goeth not out by night. She layeth her hands to the spindle, and her hands hold the distaff. She stretcheth out her hand to the poor; yea, she reacheth forth her hands to the needy. She is not afraid of the snow for her household: for all her household are clothed with scarlet. She maketh herself coverings of tapestry; her clothing is silk and purple. Her husband is known in the gates, when he sitteth among the elders of the land. She maketh fine linen, and selleth it; and delivereth girdles unto the merchant. Strength and honour are her clothing; and she shall rejoice in time to come. She openeth her mouth with wisdom; and in her tongue is the law of kindness. She looketh well to the ways of her household, and eateth not the bread of idleness. Her children arise up, and call her blessed; her husband also, and he praiseth her. Many daughters have done virtuously, but thou excellest them all. Favour is deceitful, and beauty is vain: but a woman that feareth the LORD, she shall be praised. Give her of* *the fruit of her hands; and let her own works praise her in the gates.*

He showed me that my worth was all based on the reality of who I am in Him, and in my ability to obey His commands. I had to learn that I was my husband's helper and my son's mentor.

Titus 2:5 *- The aged women likewise, that they be in behaviour as becometh holiness, not false accusers, not given to much wine, teachers of good things; That they may teach the young women to be sober, to love their husbands, to love their children, To be discreet, chaste, keepers at home, good, obedient to their own husbands, that the word of God be not blasphemed.*

I was placed on earth, first of all, to love my husband and make his life easier by helping him to succeed. Secondly, I am commanded to raise God-fearing children, to carry on His work in this world. It is easy, as a woman, to feel that God is not fair in His expectations of us...until, we understand what we were created for. If you try to use a hammer to remove a screw, you will certainly destroy the furniture you are working on. Either, you need to use a screwdriver and remove the screw, or you need to use the hammer to drive down nails elsewhere. Only then, will you see a beautiful and useful piece of furniture, fit for the use it was intended for. I needed to remember what kind of "tool" God created me to be, and then, work at the job I was designed to master. I would never be perfect at it; however, this thinking was absolutely crucial to becoming the wife and mother that God wanted me to be.

(The following is an email that my friend, Michelle, wrote in response to her friend's question, "Why in the world did you want to have kids?")

For as long as I can remember, I've always wanted kids. I've always wanted to be a mom – either naturally, or by adoption. In fact, when I was younger, there was a time when I wanted to run an orphanage or have a home for abused kids. I may have an ultra-nurturing side. I don't know. Some of this may be due to the fact that I frequently babysat for a friend of the family, who was a foster mom and had all kinds of kids, with all kinds of devastating stories, staying at her house. I always thought that having children of my own would be fun – kind of an excuse to re-live your own youth. In fact, "the more the better" was pretty much my philosophy (like "Cheaper by the Dozen – my theme movie for a time).

When I was pregnant for the first time, being a parent took on a whole new side. This was the part where a mom-to-be can experience God's miracle of life. It is difficult to explain how the amazing transformation that is happening within the belly affects the notion of "whether this is just a fetus or a real baby." I don't know where you stand on the topic of abortion, but from the very first ultrasound at about

6 or 8 weeks – you can actually see this little peanut of a baby moving around. From this point, there was absolutely no turning back and there was only the anticipation of what was to come.

So, now as we deal with pee in the beds, milk running out of our noses, being up all night with a sick kid, and pulling broccoli out of the fish bowl, we often wonder about that same question, *"Why in the world did we want to have kids?!?!?!?!?"* It's really simple.

First, I consider that the joys definitely outnumber the temper tantrums. Watching them reach those first milestones – sitting up, walking, running, running away, trying to climb the Christmas tree, sharing in the sense of accomplishment when they learn something new, and just the humor in the cute and innocent things they say. "The joys of parenthood" is a phrase that is probably over-used, but it really is a joy. It's all worth it at the end of the day, when I get smothered with suffocating hugs and slobbery kisses. It's a privilege that God has allowed us to have children of our own, which sort of leads into the second reason....

Second, we both wanted to take on the responsibility of having kids. It's a huge responsibility. HUGE. Of course, there is a little of the financial responsibility, but I'm talking more of the moral responsibility. In the Bible it states:

> **Proverbs 22:6** - *Train up a child in the way he should go: and when he is old, he will not depart from it.*

Depending on how we raise our kids (and their own innate ability), we could have a future engineer, a teacher, a missionary, a professional athlete, or on the same token, we could have a "druggie," a murderer, or a hooker. We have the responsibility to steer our children into making wise everyday decisions that will eventually help build their character. If we, as parents, fail at providing the moral instruction, who knows where they will end up. In a sense, this was our combined desire to "coach."

If you're not whole-heartedly willing to accept the responsibility of children, you may want to reconsider. I once knew a guy who had a daughter with a former girl-friend. At the time that I was seeing him, his daughter was about 10 years old – a beautiful, very smart girl, who had a lot of friends and was involved in sports and other groups at school. In his own words, he described his daughter as a "financial burden." He was sore at the fact that he had to pay child support and part of the medical bills for her braces. He said that he "can't wait until she turns 18, and then he won't have the pay $50/week anymore." A bright young girl like this really deserves a decent father – a father who would want to be involved in her upbringing.

Third, we were willing to sacrifice. If someone is not willing to sacrifice, I would say not to bother having children. The word "sacrifice" holds a few different facets for us. On one side, we had the financial sacrifice. Obviously, having kids costs money. I'm not just speaking of the endless diapers, formula, clothing, and other material needs. More so, I'm talking about the change of employment and household income. If I wanted to go back to work full-time, we would have to pay for daycare for 2 children (astronomical, and not worth it). Thank God, my Mom lives nearby and can watch them 3 days a week for me. Otherwise, I would probably be a stay-at-home-mom. There isn't anything wrong or menial about being a stay-at-home-mom, just a loss of potential income.

There is also a sacrifice of our own selfishness. The same way that a man and woman must compromise parts of their "single nature" in order for a marriage to work, the same holds true for a couple wishing to share their home with a child. We have learned to tolerate Mickey Mouse Clubhouse instead of watching Rachel Ray. We have turned down meeting with friends for wine tours, house parties, and just going out and having fun and instead replaced it with reading the same Clifford book 6 times in a row and eating macaroni and cheese for dinner. Yes, there are times that we get babysitters, so we can go out and enjoy life without the kiddos, but it's definitely not often or at the drop of a hat, like we could before. We can't watch graphic or violent shows on TV, when the kids are in the room. We have to sometimes run our schedules around their naptime. We may just have to buy the Dora yogurt instead of Dannon. Some of these compromises are bigger than others, but so far, it's been well worth it.

Fourth, I would have to say that we were/are willing to accept the unexpected. While pregnant, all kinds of thoughts were going through my head as to whether or not our babies would be "normal." There are all kinds of genetic disorders out there, and were we willing to try to raise a child with a handicap? We have been very fortunate so far, but as we are now trying for another child, and I'm 36 years old, the chances of a genetic problem increase with every year. A friend of mine has a brother and sister-in-law, who were pregnant this past year with a baby diagnosed with Trisomy 18. If you don't know what that is, look it up, and you will have a good cry, I promise you. They were hoping to at least carry the baby to term and savor every moment with him, but unfortunately, God took him before he was born. Bob and I decided that we would be willing to raise a baby, regardless of constraints, either mental or physical. We also know that any day, our girls could be diagnosed with some sort of cancer, become injured in a car accident, or suffer some other impairment, that could alter their functionability. There is a boy at our church, who was a normal kid, up until age 6, when a car accident took both of his parents and his baby sister to heaven, and left him with permanent brain damage and some physical limitations. It would be difficult, but I think we are both willing to accept and work though an unexpected circumstance. I'll tell you, hearing stories like this just makes me appreciate every single crazy moment with my kids a little more.

It is very difficult to explain in a few words why we wanted to have kids, and I feel that there is a whole lot more that I'm missing. To sum it up: we are fortunate and we are blessed to have our children. I really can't imagine life without them. Parenting is definitely a learning experience, and there isn't anyone, other than Bob, who I would want to take the "course" with. I have the best partner to help raise our kids!

I asked Bob this same question (why he wanted to have kids). His answer: "I wanted someone to play with." That's all he had to say.

Michelle

L ester and I got married in April, 2001 hoping to start a family right away. After a year of trying to conceive our first child, we had many tests done to see if there were any problems. All tests came back normal - unexplained infertility. The doctors referred us to a fertility clinic, but after praying about it- we decided to leave it in God's hands. I went to the doctor for a check-up after one year of marriage to discover a lump on my thyroid. It was biopsied and found to be cancer. After having my thyroid removed, it was determined it was not cancerous. I now take daily thyroid meds and get checked regularly for thyroid issues. Was this the cause of infertility?

Six long, difficult years passed of waiting on God's perfect timing. I turned 40 and thought my days of fertility had passed by, but God had other plans. I took a pregnancy test one month after turning 40 and it was positive! We were so excited! The excitement was short lived, when on Easter Sunday, I started to bleed. We went to the doctor who confirmed we had experienced our first miscarriage at 6 weeks. We were devastated, yet hopeful, because after six years of unexplained infertility, we were able to get pregnant. We rested on the following verse:

Jeremiah 29:11 - *"For I know the plans I have for you, declares the Lord, plans for welfare and not for evil, to give you a future and a hope."*

A few months later we were pregnant again. The first ultrasound showed a wonderful beating heart, and we were so excited! Unfortunately, at 8 weeks, when we went for our second ultrasound, that lovely heartbeat had stopped. We were so crushed!! I had a D&C and we sent our baby off for tests to figure out a possible cause of miscarriage. It was a boy, who we named "Jacob," and he had Trisomy 13 - an extra #13 chromosome. We turned to God as our refuge and strength, and gave it to the Lord that if he wanted us to be parents, then He would allow it to happen.

Psalm 27:14 - *"Wait for the Lord, be strong, and let your heart take courage, Wait for the Lord!"*

Six months went by, and each month I wondered if I could possibly be pregnant again. Yes, the test came back positive, but we were very cautious about getting excited. I gave 7 vials of blood to see if there were any issues that had not been discovered yet. I found out I have Factor V Leiden - my blood tends to clot more, due to not reacting to Protein C. I was put on a daily aspirin routine to help thin my blood. The first ultrasound revealed a beautiful beating heart, and a few weeks later, another wonderful ultrasound. Things were looking up! I was so positive that pregnancy number 3 was going to be a full-term baby. It is amazing how your whole life can change in a matter of one minute. Unfortunately, at 11 weeks, at our 3rd ultrasound, the heart was no longer beating. Déjà vu again! A D&C was done and the baby sent for tests again. We once again, had a precious baby boy we named "Matthew." He had a Trisomy 15 - an extra #15 chromosome.

I wrote in my journal in the hospital, "This loss has made us realize that maybe the Lord doesn't want us to have a biological child. I'm 41 and can't go through this again- 3 miscarriages in the span of one year are just too much for me to handle. We might seek adoption down the road, but right now, I just need to heal. I'm so thankful for my precious husband, family, and friends!"

I continued keeping busy with my teaching and friends, trying not to dwell on not being able to have my heart's desire - a biological child. Eleven months later, I went to the dentist. They wanted to take X-rays but my intuition told me I might be pregnant. The hygienist said, "Okay, when I see you in six months, we'll see if your instincts are correct." I immediately went home and took a pregnancy test- it was NEGATIVE! Once again I was totally crushed and so devastated.

One week went by, and I still had not gotten my period, so I nonchalantly took a pregnancy test. My husband walked by the test while he was talking on the phone and about dropped the phone in the sink- it was POSITIVE! Whoa! My instincts were correct, but I was so cautious about getting excited. The doctor did blood work and sent us for a 6 week ultrasound. It was such a beautiful sight to see a beating heart, yet again. Since the pregnancy was now viable, I was put on Lovenox shots once a day to help thin my blood. Yes, every night my wonderful husband gave me a shot in my stomach. At eight weeks, we had another ultrasound and saw a beating heart and a waving baby. It was so cute, like my baby was saying, "See you in 7 months Mommy."

The pregnancy went smoothly, considering I was advanced maternal age (hate that term) and high-risk, due to miscarriages and Factor V Leiden. I had to go to the high-risk doctor several times. At 30 weeks, I was diagnosed with gestational diabetes so I had to take my blood sugars 4 times a day and watch what I ate. Fortunately, I was able to control it with diet and did not need insulin shots. I jokingly tell people it saved me from gaining too much weight.

At 39 weeks and 3 days, we went to the hospital to be induced at 8pm. My water broke at 5:15am, got an epidural at 9:30am, started pushing at 11:45am, and had our precious miracle baby at 12:27pm. It was so amazing! Most doctors discourage ladies over 40 to have a baby. Well, in my case, I have been more fertile (4 pregnancies) in my 40's than in any other time of my life. God is in the miracle business! We are so blessed to have been given this precious child to raise! Thank you Lord!

Mary Lombard
Leesburg, Georgia

Chapter 2

The Miracle of Pregnancy

In the summer of 2009, my husband and I were re-arranging our living room, when the subject of having another child came up, which was a bit of a surprise to both of us. Previously, we had talked about waiting until our first child would be entering pre-school. I thought it would be nice to spend a lot of one-on-one time with each of my babies. However, it seemed that both of us had been thinking the same thing. The older Channing got, the more we felt that he needed some companionship. We knew it would take a bit longer to get pregnant this time, as I was still using birth control. So, I set up an appointment to see Dr. Miller, that March. From the day that the contraceptive was removed, I began having many symptoms of pregnancy. This was attributed to the hormonal changes going on in my body, but needless to say, in my anticipation, I wasted quite a few pregnancy tests during those first few months.

In July, we finally had a positive test. It was very faint, but still positive. In my research, I read that a false positive is quite unlikely, as the test is only designed to work when the pregnancy hormone is detected. The following day, I took another test. It was positive again, but even fainter. This was definitely a red flag to me. I had certainly not neglected to read about ectopic pregnancy, miscarriage, and a thousand other things that could go wrong. As God would have it, I only had about a week to think about all of the possibilities, however. The following Tuesday night (I believe it was the 9th), I began bleeding quite heavily followed by very painful cramping. I narrowly escaped a midnight adventure in the emergency room, and called my doctor the following morning. I had blood work done several days later, but the hormone was no longer in my system. Further reading led me to believe that I may have had a "chemical pregnancy." This is when the egg implants in the uterus, but it only remains attached long enough to allow a small amount of the pregnancy hormone to be released into your system, before falling off. Most women dismiss this as a late period, so many of these pregnancies go unaccounted for. I don't really think that this loss affected me much at the time. We had only *just* gotten the positive test. There was not much time to let things "sink in," so it seemed pretty easy to just "move on." So, after a quick cry, that's what I did. I definitely did not realize it at the time, but this is when God began an amazing work in my life. The next couple of years would be full of spiritual and emotional growth. Eventually, due to life's twists and turns, I would come to cherish this microscopic human as a start of "showers of blessings" from the hand of God. Though many of these "showers" were painful while going through them, they allowed for awesome displays of God's faithfulness and grace to grow in my life. Looking back on this time, about a year and a half later, I decided to call this baby, "Blessing."

I continued to experience pregnancy symptoms, but by now, I was getting used to it. In late September 2009, I noticed an increase in my symptoms again. So, at the beginning of October, I took another test. This one was positive in about 30 seconds and much more pronounced. I decided to tell Kevin about it on his birthday, the 7th, and I placed the positive test in an envelope with a ribbon on it, as a gift for him. After opening it, he took one very quick look at it and asked me why I gave it to him. I just stared at him in disbelief, wondering if he was joking or if; after seeing "several hundred" of these tests, he still did not know how to read it. I guess men truly don't take hints well. He had not looked close enough, and he said that he thought it was negative. Leave it to a man! I'm not sure why he thought I would give him a negative one, but hey, what woman really understands how men process things, right? Anyhow, our excitement began to mount, once again. After several more "very" positive home-pregnancy tests, I made my appointment for the usual recommended blood work. Everything came back normal, and we scheduled our first appointment and ultrasound for the middle of November. After months of trying, it seemed like all of our wishing and hoping and dreaming was finally becoming a reality.

There were a few things about pregnancy that really struck me during those "odd" months of being pregnant. First of all, I found that it is so easy to forget how precious and fragile each life really is.

Psalm 144:4 - Man is like to vanity: his days are as a shadow that passeth away.

Because of my health issues, when I was pregnant with Channing, I had made a "rule" for myself to enjoy every moment, as if it were the only chance I would ever have. What an incredible blessing it was to do so, because at this point, I was still not sure that I would ever carry another child full-term. God controls the "if," "when," and "how" of each pregnancy. I do not have control over how my pregnancy will progress. I was learning to appreciate each and every moment with the miracle of a new life growing inside me. It is easy to feel "cheated" when you never have a chance to hold that little life, but only by God's discretion is a child born into this world and given to us to care for. It truly made me appreciate Channing so much more, and thankful for every minute I was given with him. It sure made those long nights falling asleep in the rocking chair and waking with a stiff neck much more bearable.

> ***Proverbs 9:11*** *- For by me thy days shall be multiplied, and the years of thy life shall be increased.*

Secondly, life truly does begin at conception. The heart starts beating just 22 days after conception, which is before most women even know that they are pregnant! This should encourage us to value the sanctity of life even more, especially as Christian parents. The Bible says that God pre-ordained each life, before it was even formed in the womb. If we believe that life starts at conception, then, we must believe that a spirit is placed in each unborn child at that time as well. (This fact and some prompting from family members and friends led me to do some research, and I've come to the conclusion that I can no longer support the use of the majority of common birth-control methods. This would be another book in and of itself, but to make a long story short, most of them can cause spontaneous abortions. Most likely, you will not find this in any information that you have, but you will need to ask your doctor for additional information from the company, printed in a separate booklet. If you use or have formerly used birth-control methods, I would urge you to do some research, before using it again or recommending it to someone else.)

> ***Psalm 139:13-16 (English Standard Version)*** *- For you formed my inward parts; you knitted me together in my mother's womb. I praise you, for I am fearfully and wonderfully made. Wonderful are your works; my soul knows it very well. My frame was not hidden from you, when I was being made in secret, intricately woven in the depths of the earth. Your eyes saw my unformed substance; in*

your book were written, every one of them, the days that were formed for me, when as yet there was none of them.

Jeremiah 1:5a - *Before I formed thee in the belly I knew thee; and before thou camest forth out of the womb I sanctified thee...*

God has chosen the perfect combination for each child – unique DNA, eye color, hair color, sex, etc. God's plan is always perfect. If I had become pregnant one day later, Channing would have been entirely different. The thought is so amazing and humbling. Only God knows what He is doing and why He is doing it. I must learn to trust His timing in my life. It is truly worth the wait!

Another very important fact that was impressed upon me during this time was the absolute necessity of being within the perfect will of God. It is so easy, as humans, to assume that we know what we want. However, if we take the time to meditate on God and who He is, it should not take long for us to realize that His ways are truly not our ways. He sees the beginning and the end of all things, so why would we not trust Him to lead us in the very best direction for our life?

Isaiah 55:9 - *For as the heavens are higher than the earth, so are my ways higher than your ways, and my thoughts than your thoughts.*

His timing is not our timing either. Time is a concept that He created for us. He does not need the constraint of time, nor does He operate within the boundaries of time, like we do.

II Peter 3:8 - *But, beloved, be not ignorant of this one thing, that one day is with the Lord as a thousand years, and a thousand years as one day.*

He knows the perfect plan for each of us, and I truly believe that if we think about it long enough, we will find that we would much rather be within that perfect will, than outside of it. There is a certain fear that I have come to know, when I contemplate my life without the leading and direction of my Heavenly Father. His ways are truly best, and I am learning to trust in that fact and that alone.

I guess that it is only human for us to get wrapped up in the little "bubble" that we call our lives. We make rash judgments and quick decisions about who we are, who God is, and what we want in our lives. It is just so easy to forget the absolute miracle of each life, especially when a pregnancy becomes difficult and painful. We forget that each life – not just ours, but the baby's as well - is a gift from God, designed and ordained by His hand. When we surrender completely to the plan of God, we will find the necessary strength, in Him, to do what He asks us to do, even when it feels impossible.

Ephesians 2:10 - For we are his workmanship, created in Christ Jesus unto good works, which God hath before ordained that we should walk in them.

For all of my life, as long as I can remember, I have wanted to be a mom. God gave us Isaac, our son through the beautiful blessing of adoption, and let me become a mom on this earth. I will forever thank Him for that. However, another thing that some may think weird, is that I wanted to experience being pregnant long enough to feel my baby move, to see the beautiful baby outline on the ultrasound machine, to hear the precious heart beating, to find out if it's a boy or a girl, and to experience labor and birthing my own baby. I researched and researched, and I wanted to have a natural delivery - with a midwife, at the hospital, and using a doula to help with relaxation techniques, various positions, and massages to help get me through it. I wanted no epidurals, and wanted to feel all the pain of bringing my baby into this world. I know many think that is crazy, but it's something I've always wanted to do. Though, Annabelle is home now and not still with us, God blessed me with so many gifts, while being pregnant with her. He answered so many of my prayers, that I cannot help but praise Him and write about it.

We found out on February 13th, 2011 that we were expecting. I woke up in the middle of the night, took a pregnancy test, and practically burst through the door to show Jim, who was still trying to wake up and figure out what

I was doing. Then, I called my mom, in the middle of the night/early morning, to tell her the news too. At that time, we didn't hope for much, since we had miscarried 4 times before during the first trimester. We decided that, even though the outcome might be bad and we would probably miscarry again, we would praise God and be excited for whatever time we had with our baby. Our first appointment was just two days later, and they confirmed with a positive result. From that point on, we went to normal appointments, and everything began wonderfully. We got to see her at just 6 weeks, 3 days on ultrasound, when she looked more like a little blob, but oh, so adorable and precious to us. Her heart rate was in the 190's. Around 10-12 weeks, I started to spot a little, so we would go in every few days for a heartbeat check, and an ultrasound. What a blessing that was, because for the first time, we didn't just get to *see* the heart beating but we *heard* it too. It was one of the most precious things we've ever heard. We even have a recording of it on our phone, along with a recording of the ultrasound they did, when she was just 11 weeks old. She was bouncing around on the screen, moving her legs, and waving at us. We had never gotten far enough to see our baby actually *look* like a baby. It was an amazing, joyous day for us, and one we will never forget.

We were so excited, when the bleeding finally stopped. Around that time, we also began to finally tell everyone. It was the most amazing thing to us that we finally made it out of the first trimester and into the second one. We had never done that before. We were finally feeling like this might be it. We might actually get to keep this baby. I started to get some maternity clothes, and we started thinking about all the things we would have to get done before her arrival. It was an exciting time. Everything was looking wonderful through the first part of the second trimester. At every appointment, we would laugh with the midwife and doctors, as they would try to hear her heart beating, but she would give them such a hard time. She moved around so much. They would hear it, and then, she would move and they would have to move again. Finally, after about 5 minutes, she would show off and come up closer, allowing us to hear her heartbeat strong and loud. It was always between 160-170, which made us think she was a girl, even from the start.

Everything was going wonderful. We were so thrilled! I started showing, and LOVED it! I had never gotten to experience that before. I loved watching my belly grow, knowing a life was growing inside of it. Right before we left for Florida to visit family, we had our gender ultrasound at 18 weeks, 5 days. She was so healthy and perfect on the ultrasound. She was even measuring ahead at 19 weeks, 2 days. The doctor showed us that our baby had three lines - it was a girl, and we were so excited! The thought of Isaac having a little sister and being able to buy so many cute "girly" things - made me so happy. I began to feel her move more - which is another thing I always wanted to experience. We were able to get a great family picture of us standing by a waterfall-fountain-type thing that I will always treasure, because we are all four together, even though she was in my tummy. It doesn't matter. She was alive and well and growing inside me.

I really started popping out around weeks 19-20. I just loved looking at my tummy and thinking about my baby girl growing in there. We ordered the crib and her beautiful green and pink bedding, and we were just about to do the nursery the following week. On Thursday, the 2nd, I started to spot/bleed some, and it scared me. So, my midwife told us go to St. Ann's to get checked out. They were amazing, and did so many tests. That night, everything was great. We had the chance to see our beautiful baby girl again on the screen, and to hear her heart beating again - which was wonderful! My cervix was closed, and they could not figure out why I was bleeding lightly, so they sent me home with instructions to follow-up on Tuesday with my midwife/doctor's office. We felt good knowing baby girl was fine and that, hopefully, the bleeding would just go away. We thought it was starting to, but instead, it changed, and some other stuff started coming out too. That kind of scared me. Then, on Sunday morning, during church, I started cramping. I left and went home to lay down. It was sporadic and not too painful, but I was scared now, knowing I was bleeding lightly *and* cramping. Finally, I called my midwife that night, and we went back down to St. Ann's.

All was going well, and we heard heart beating right away, which made us very happy. So we were just sitting there, talking with the doctor, while she was doing a cervical check, thinking everything was okay. Then, all of a sudden, she looked up, her face completely changed, and said there were some membranes poking out, when she inserted the speculum. She explained that it was part of the amniotic sac. I was also dilated 2 cm. She told me that they would admit me, and I would lay in a trendelenburg position all night, to try to help the amniotic sac go back up into the uterus. I would be evaluated in the morning, to see if they could do a cerclage, or if I would have to deliver our baby. They explained that the baby would not be able to survive, because she would need at least a few more weeks, before they could even do anything to try to help her. There are no words to describe what came over me, and how I felt at that moment. From that moment, until after I gave birth to her, I put myself on a kind of "autopilot" and shut off the tears. I knew I needed to keep my body as relaxed as possible and be strong for her.

I could not sleep the entire night, even with sleep medication. I finally cat-napped around 5 or 6 am, and started to have contractions around 7:00ish. I woke Jim up, and the day began. Just a little later, the doctors and such came in to evaluate me. The contractions were getting worse. At first, they thought that I was fully dilated, but later realized that it was the amniotic sac coming down further, and I was really only 3 cm. However, my body was naturally going into labor, and there was nothing they could do. We were told that we would have to deliver her. At that point, I felt kind of numb and just went into this "I have to do this, so let's just do it" mode, where I just focused on the task at hand, realizing that I had to go through it. I knew I wanted pictures. We called a friend, who is a professional photographer, and she took time out of her day to come, wait, and take pictures of our precious Annabelle for us. We also wanted to see Annabelle one more time, while she was alive and well, kicking and moving, and her heart was beating, in my tummy. We asked if they would do an ultrasound just for us. They did, and they were amazing. They brought it right into the room, and even our parents and my sister got to watch with Jim and me, as we saw Annabelle alive for the last time. We recorded it on our phone, along with the last recording of her heart beating - something I will always cherish.

At the beginning of my labor, I told them that because I was emotionally in so much pain, that I didn't think I wanted to experience physical pain as well, so they gave me some IV meds - just enough to take the edge off and help me get some rest in-between contractions, by closing my eyes and relaxing. However, towards the end of my labor, they didn't work. The only thing that would work at that time was an epidural, but I didn't want one, so I just breathed through the contractions and rested in-between.

The doctor from the office had to deliver Annabelle, since I was pre-term, but my wonderful midwife still stuck around to help me through it. Labor and delivery was something I wanted to document and to write about, because I have always wanted to know what it felt like to bring my baby into this world. God gave me that gift, and I will always remember it. Jim told me, afterwards, that he could not have been prouder of me, and that no one could take the moment of birthing Annabelle away from me. Jim was just amazing through it all. In all the pictures, right after delivery, you can see his hand on me in all of them. I could go on and on about him and how amazing he was and how he is the best father in the whole world, but it would take too many pages. I am so thankful for the opportunity to have had labored and birthed Annabelle. I know that not everyone who gives birth to a baby is able to experience it - due to complications that may arise, c-sections, or an epidural. The doctor wanted to give me Pitocin to speed up labor and help Annabelle out, but my midwife asked if we could do some natural things first for stimulation of the uterus. We did, and it worked some. The doctor still wanted to try Pitocin, so we started the Pitocin. At this point of labor, the contractions started getting much worse. The IV meds had worn off completely, and I felt everything. I have heard so many times that even women that want a natural birth, but who have to end up having Pitocin, many times get an epidural, just because the Pitocin increases the pain so much more than it naturally would be without Pitocin. I was worried, but I made it through until the very end. It was so intense, that I asked for an epidural, but they let me know I was very close. They thought I could do it. My midwife was amazing, and coached me through it – she kept telling me that I could do it. It really helped. I am SO thankful that I never got the epidural, and even with Pitocin-intense contractions, I labored and birthed my baby girl. Again, this will be something I'll never forget.

I wondered how I would do, since we never got to take our Bradley natural method birthing classes, and I didn't have my doula there. Thankfully, all of the reading that I did paid off. So many of the things I had read, about how it might feel, turned out true for me, and it made me excited, knowing that I was getting to experience this. I started to get contractions that were so intense that they started to go into my butt. I remember saying how bad my butt hurt, which I knew was right before you need to push. I couldn't wait any longer. Everyone was rushing in, and I was just waiting for them to say "go," because I was completely ready. My body naturally let me know when it was ready to push her out. It's something that I'll never forget. I remembered exactly how to push from reading. Afterwards, they told me I pushed perfectly. I never felt tension or straining anywhere in my body, except exactly where it needed to be. It was as if you were pushing out a big bowel movement. I focused on exactly the point in my body that needed to push, and I just did it. It was the worst pain of my life, but now looking back, I loved it, because I was laboring for my Annabelle. I was birthing her, and I will never forget that. I am so thankful that I got to experience every single pain of bringing her into this world. I remember the exact moment she came into this world, after around 3 or so pushes, because I felt the immediate gush/ release of her body and the immediate feeling of no more pain. From that moment on, I had no more pain. It amazed me how immediately it went away, after she came out. We requested for her to be brought right up to me on my chest, so as soon as the doctor cut the cord and clamped it, she was brought up to my chest for Jim and I to see. I am so thankful my mom was there, because she has a picture of Annabelle right after she came out, still attached to her umbilical cord. I love this, because a part of her was still connected to me. Annabelle Cherrea Starkey was born on June 6, 2011 at 4:42 pm weighing 13.3 precious ounces and was 10.2 inches long.

We were amazed at how tiny she was, and yet, how perfectly formed she was. Right away, the doctor and midwife commented how perfect she was. I thought at first they were just being nice, but after getting her report back and reading how she had no anomalies and nothing wrong with her, I realized that they actually meant it. She was perfect and formed just exactly right, but just was too small to survive on her own. We were looking at her for a moment, and I asked if she was still alive. We couldn't see her heart beating through her chest or the cord pulsating, so we decided she was already with Jesus. Since she was healthy and alive in my womb, I am guessing it was either the trauma of birthing her out, or cutting the cord that determined the timing that she went home.

We took our time, as we cried tears of joy and sorrow. Jim and I were the proudest parents I think you'll ever meet. I remember Jim just standing there in awe of her and crying. He and I were just touching and checking out each and every little part of her. Jim didn't know she would be so formed, so it was such a blessing and gift to him to see every little knuckle bone and ankle bone and to feel her ribs and see her little ears. I then noticed how she had his big gap between her big toe and the one beside it, just like him. Her feet shaped exactly like Daddy's. We went on to realize that she had my nose, lips, and hands and Jim's eyes and feet. She even had the little dent in her chin, just like Jim and I do. We were amazed at how she already had soft hair on her head, and little eyebrows growing in. Her eyes were not opened yet, so we were so thankful to know the first thing she saw when she opened her eyes, was her Savior. We can only imagine what that must have been like for her.

We each held her, cried over her, and talked to her, for what felt like forever. I sang to her, and though I cannot remember all the songs, I do remember singing "How can I keep from singing" by Chris Tomlin and "I will carry you" by Selah to her. We felt so thankful to have had this time with her. Our family came in, and her grandparents got to see and hold her, along with her Aunt Monica. We brought Isaac in, and we had some family pictures done with him and her, after we introduced him to his baby sister. It was a sweet time. After everyone left, Jim and I held her, said our last little bits and prayed with her, holding each other, and thanking God for her. We prayed for strength to let her go. How awesome to know that as we were praying to Him and holding our baby girl, He was holding her too. She was home.

That is when I let the flood gates open, and from then on, they haven't stopped. We love her so much, and she will always be missed and loved. A piece was missing from our hearts, that will not be filled, until we see her again, when we are all together with our Savior. We found out that we were able to see her the next day. The hospital was so amazing, giving us so many beautiful keepsakes. We also found out that we could even take her with us to the funeral home. So on the hour drive, I got to hold her in my arms, and sing to her. When we got there, we had to face the hardest thing we had to do so far. We pulled in the parking lot and stopped the car. We held each other, while we each had a hand on her, and Jim and I both prayed. God carried us through, and helped us give her to the funeral directors, knowing that that would be the last time we saw her precious face, while we are on this earth.

So we grieve, but we grieve with hope. We know we will see her again. We got to spend a "little while" with Annabelle, and we will have a "little while" where we will be apart. The next time we see our precious Annabelle, we will be together forever with our Savior. I will cling to that! Thank you, God, for the "little while."

The following quote reminds us that even though her life was short, we are so blessed that God picked us to be her parents. For some reason, that we won't understand this side of heaven, He picked us to be Annabelle's parents. He also picked her to leave this world early, so that He could do a mighty work through her short life, for His kingdom. He has a purpose for her life, and He will bring good from it. I cannot wait until the day when all things are new and we see everything unfolded. We will be home together with

Annabelle, our four other children, and with our Savior, and we will worship Him forever.

> "The amount of time on earth matters very little: a man can live in greed and pride 90 years and never find God, know Him, or accomplish His plan. A stillborn baby on the other hand, teaches people to love, brings people to the Lord, teaches us the tenuous nature of life and teaches us a faith that those who have not suffered loss can never know. A child not even breathing for an hour, can have an impact greater than a famous preacher. The purpose of a life is not ours to decide nor in our hands: it is brought about by God" – Author Unknown

Annabelle's name means "grace." We have seen that worked out so much through this pregnancy. By God's grace, we were able to get pregnant with her in the first place. By God's grace, we were able to feel her move. By God's grace we were able to get as far along as we did in the pregnancy. By God's grace we were able to spend precious time with our sweet Annabelle. By God's grace we are slowly, minute by minute, making it through this journey, and by God's grace and because of what Christ did on the cross, we know without a doubt we will see her again one day, after seeing our Savior face to face. Until that day, we will miss her every day, but we will hold onto the hope, knowing that that day will come, when we will see Annabelle again. Then, we will be able to hold her, and be with her and our other children, along with our Savior. All things will be made new, and we will all be together forever to worship our Savior. So, as the days ahead will be hard for us, and that many times it will be hard to breathe, we will cling to that hope and the promises of our Sovereign God, and we will thank Him for the "little while" that we had with her. Though such a short time, it was a precious, beautiful time that we will never forget and that we will always treasure.

I you would like to read more about our family and our journey, please feel free to visit our blog www.starkeyfami-lythree.blogspot.com.

April Starkey
Mansfield, Ohio

-◈┥ **Chapter 3** ┝◈-

The Miracle of Children

I guess that I have spent my life filled with such a desire to have children that I never really felt the need to remind myself of the amazing blessing that comes with each one. I think that maybe I just felt that sacrificial love, patience, and understanding would just come naturally when the baby "popped" out. I sure had another thing coming.

Allow me to revisit my first pregnancy for a moment. I can still remember my labor with Channing like it was yesterday. They say you forget all of the pain as soon as your baby is in your arms, but I beg to differ. I was induced a week early, due to my back problems. I had figured that I would just go "drug-free" since I was "used to pain," and I figured that nothing could be as awful as a back spasm that knocks you to the floor. Well...another lesson in my naivety. (I was beginning to see why God compares us to sheep!) Anyhow, let me just say that January 29, 2008 was probably one of the worst days of my life. (Not that the birth of my child was not a wonderful moment in my life, but just bear with me for a minute.) I was induced, first thing that morning, after having spent a short and uneventful night at the hospital. The first couple of hours were a breeze. Then, all of a sudden, the real pain began. I could tell that my patience was getting shorter, and I dismissed everyone except for my husband. I did not want anyone else seeing me in whatever condition I ended in, or the journey it took to get there. It had, undoubtedly, begun.

In past generations, women were usually encouraged to walk the halls or just lay in bed, during labor. Well, that was then…this was now. I was asked to crawl, squat, bounce on an exercise ball, and other such uncomfortable things. I could hardly do half of those things on a good day, but with the added 45 pounds, cramping legs, varicose veins, impatient bladder, contractions, headache, and nauseousness, it was nearly hilarious…well, for someone watching, maybe. (Doesn't that make pregnancy and labor sound really romantic?) I felt like a whale who got thrown on a unicycle, which then went racing in circles over numerous potholes, until I couldn't see straight anymore. It was the wildest ride I have ever had or will ever care to have again!

About 10 hours into labor, I was begging for a giant needle to be stabbed into my back. Unfortunately, an epidural was out of the question for me, due to my degenerative spine. I did not realize that the anesthesiologist would want current MRIs or at least some prior medical records, and of course, no one offered that information until my screams were echoing down the hospital halls. The nurses gave me fentanyl in my IV, but it only dulled the pain for about 5 minutes. I think it was in those 5 minutes that I had time to get a little delirious. I just remember mumbling "lincoln logs," before being jolted back into reality, with another stabbing contraction. That was the only "deep and thought-provoking" thing that I said all day, and no one even heard it! The rest of the time was filled with screams of "God, help me," "I'm scared," "I can't do this anymore," and "I'm going to throw up." Needless to say, a vast number of people heard *those* things over and over for several hours. At least I was being honest, and thankfully, I never got mean, yelled at my husband (except when he tried to offer me some ice cream mid-contraction, because it was "so good!"), or swore, as some women do. I just utterly terrified an entire wing of nervous women, about to face the same fate at any moment. I am guessing that a majority of them took the epidural, even if they had not planned on it...so much for their birth plan!

Little Channing Mark entered the world at 9:07pm on January 29, 2008. It was a long day. Kevin and I took a couple of minutes, while I held him, to thank God for our new little blessing, and then, the "party" started. I called one person after another on the cell phone, while those, who had patiently sat in the waiting room all day, passed Channing around. Earlier, I had said that it was one of the worst days of my life. This is considering that I did not really have a chance to spend more than five minutes with my little guy, until 1:30am the *next* morning. After the nurse finally wheeled in the bassinet, Kevin stayed for a couple of minutes and then, headed off to let our two dogs out and get some much-deserved sleep. The nurse handed me my baby boy, and told me not to fall asleep with him. So, I dutifully remained awake the rest of the night. (I had no idea that I could send him to the nursery, and maybe they were already inundated, because they did not offer the information either.) I look back now, and those were some of the best hours of my life. I can still see that beautiful, tiny head lifting to meet my gaze – his little blue-gray eyes, below a little crop of dark brown hair, were full of wonder and interest. With only the smallest of sounds now and then, he seemed to enjoy the quiet calm as much as I did. The miniature photocopy of my husband seemed to contain all the love that we had for each other in his little being. My miracle had arrived at last.

The next few months were very full of many things: diapers, rashes, baths, crying (mostly from me), doctors visits, constant nursing (until I felt like a vending machine in a high school break room) and of course, total and complete exhaustion. I had always been taught, or maybe it had just been inferred, that depression of any kind was *always* a spiritual problem, and as I mentioned previously, I certainly did not believe any differently about post-partum depression. The thought had crossed my mind, several times over the first nine months, after my son's birth, that my spiritual life may not be the only issue that I was struggling with. I was embarrassed to admit it to anyone, or even to ask my Christian doctors about it, for fear of being found "unholy" or "unfit" as a mother. Thankfully, I never had a desire to hurt my baby, although several times, I had to walk away from him to calm down. Unfortunately, I hurled the majority of my anger and frustrations at Kevin. A lesser husband would have left me. I was miserable inside and out. I hated myself during that time. I felt so out of control, scared, and alone. Kevin was extremely long-suffering and calm. I deeply regret many things that I thought, did, and said during that time. My mouth did a lot of damage. If I look back on that time with complete honesty, I know that hormones were definitely responsible for much of it, but I would still do anything to take back much of that time in my life. Even if the depression itself was not a spiritual problem, the way that I dealt with it seemingly was. I thank God for His grace and faithfulness.

Psalm 116:1-8 - I love the LORD, because he hath heard my voice and my supplications. Because he hath inclined his ear unto me, therefore will I call upon him as long as I live. The sorrows of death compassed me, and the pains of hell gat hold upon me: I found trouble and sorrow. Then called I upon the name of the LORD; O LORD, I beseech thee, deliver my soul. Gracious is the LORD, and righteous; yea, our God is merciful. The LORD preserveth the simple: I was brought low, and he helped me. Return unto thy rest, O my soul; for the LORD hath dealt bountifully with thee. For thou hast delivered my soul from death, mine eyes from tears, and my feet from falling.

Finally, Kevin told me that he had had enough. I knew he would never leave me physically, but the threat that he would leave me emotionally, was just too much. He was and is my best friend, and I had hurt him deeply with my cutting words and insensitive actions. I wish I had humbled myself to get help sooner – much sooner. Finally, I found an excuse to talk to the doctor at an appointment for Channing. He was so kind and gracious. He explained that often hormones are thrown off balance, especially during and after pregnancy. He said that medication would usually help to regulate this within a couple of months or it could even take several years. I began taking an anti-depressant, and my world began to shed its shades of gray and black. For the first time, I was happy to be a new mom to my precious little boy. I was just so saddened about all the time I had "missed out" on with him. He would be a year old in a couple of short months. I had a lot of "catching up" to do.

Looking back on this "dark time" has made me aware of so much. First of all, I am learning not to take this wonderful gift of parenting lightly. I need to be continually studying and learning how to become the very best steward I can possibly be of this wonderful blessing. The Bible mentions God's love for children over and over again. He places a significant value on the way children are treated and cared for.

Luke 18:16 - *But Jesus called them unto him, and said, Suffer little children to come unto me, and forbid them not: for of such is the kingdom of God.*

Psalm 127:3 - *Lo, children are an heritage of the LORD: and the fruit of the womb is his reward.*

Mark 9:42 - *And whosoever shall offend one of these little ones that believe in me, it is better for him that a millstone were hanged about his neck, and he were cast into the sea.*

Every day we have with our children is another chance to instill values and principles that will last them a lifetime. We are entrusted with each child for a specific amount of time – whether it is one month, eighteen years, or in many cases, our entire lifetime. Only God knows the exact length of each life. From the very moment of their conception, we must put our whole heart and soul into caring for these little lives. If we truly believe that each child belongs to God, we will find it much easier to let go when God asks us to. [**Genesis 22** – *see the story of Abraham and Isaac on Mount Moriah*.] We cannot understand the ways and the mind of God. Maybe His *only* plan for some little ones is simply to glorify Himself. Possibly, He has chosen some of us to carry children just for Him. What an amazing thought! May we be found faithful in the "small" things as well as the "bigger" things of this life.

When my husband I first met, it was not long before we started talking about marriage and family. We both loved kids and knew we wanted to have a family of our own. My husband used to tease me, at first, about wanting enough kids to have his own football team. So a large family was what we were planning on. We decided to wait until our first anniversary to start trying. We wanted to enjoy the first year of just us. So our anniversary came and went, and then the years started to pass with no pregnancies.

Along the way, my cousin suggested that I might have PCOS (Poly Cystic Ovarian Syndrome), and I should talk to my family doctor about it. Being very hard to diagnose, the doctor just said it was a possibility. I took it upon myself to read up, and found that infertility was a side effect of the syndrome. So we continued to try, to no avail. I did some more research, and found a great local doctor, who specialized in women who have trouble conceiving, got the referral, and off we went to meet him. He agreed I could have PCOS, and there were a few tests we could go through to see what the problem was. I got all checked out and so did my husband. There did not seem to be anything that should be stopping me from getting pregnant. So we talked about all our options. We tried a medication to treat the symptoms of the PCOS hoping that would let my body function as it was suppose to. That went horrible, the medication made me so sick that we could not even try to make a baby.

When we had exhausted the steps we could afford, and all that was left was fertility drugs, we had a hard choice to make. All that I had read scared us, because a lot of cases lead to births of multiples. We were so afraid of ending up with what my husband lovingly referred to a "litter of babies" and selection reduction was not a choice for us. We felt (and still do) that life begins at conception, and selection reduction is killing a baby. At this point, we resigned ourselves to the fact we would never have our own children. Not unless God changed his plan for us. I know at this point in my life, I was very mad at God and blamed him for my feeling so inadequate. It took several more years of trying - to no avail - to reach my breaking point.

I remember I was driving in the car, hearing a song on the radio (not even sure what the song was now), and found myself crying. The grief over not being able to get pregnant just pouring out of me and I remember praying out loud, "God, I don't like this road you have me on, but I will trust that you have a plan for me and if it is not to be someone's mommy, then, I will accept that with your help." It was as if that was what God was waiting for me to do. Now it's not like we got pregnant the next day but over the next year or so things started to happen. I finally got an official diagnosis of PCOS, got started on a new medication they were using to help with the side effect of the PCOS, and four months after that - SURPRISE! We have a miracle: I was pregnant. A picture perfect nine months later, our son was born. My husband and I were rocked to our souls. We were so blessed, we knew it, and we continue to thank God every day for our miracle.

Just before our son turned one we started talking about trying again. I would love it if our son was not an only child, and that he could have a sibling to grow up with and share life's miracles with, as I was so fortunate to have in my sister. My husband, the more pragmatic of us, said that he would be just fine if it was not in God's plan for another baby. Another four months later, we learned God wanted us to be parents again, but something was different with this pregnancy. I, of course, feared the worst, and was sure I was going to have a miscarriage as a result of the complications I had, after my C-section for my son. I was so nervous. Let me just say that I love the saying, "God brings people into your life when you need them most." Well, God had matched us up with the best OBGYN in the area (at least in my opinion), when I got pregnant with our son. Being the great doctor he is and so compassionate for his patients, he ordered an ultrasound right away to make sure everything was okay. Everything was okay and much more. We got the surprise of a lifetime. Not only had God given us another healthy pregnancy, but He had blessed us with twin girls! We were twice as blessed.

Everything went text book perfect, until 35 weeks and our two little angels decided to make their entrance early. Instead of the planned, calm and relaxing C-section we had planned, the girls were born amidst, what can only be described as the most organized chaos possible. The scariest moment for us as parents was when our first daughter was born and did not cry right away. She was whisked out of the room, before we could hear her or even see her. When daughter number two was born, we did hear her and got a quick glance before she too was whisked away. I, the mommy, would not get to see or hold my daughters until they were a day and half old. That was excruciating, not being able to go to my new babies because I could not get out of bed. I do thank God for such wonderful family and medical staff at the hospital, because they all made sure I saw pictures of my new miracles (even though that is not the same as holding your new baby(ies) - a sorry pity party for myself). In all, the whole event was a huge reminder of how fragile life is, and how we are not in control. Only God is in control. Despite the rough entry into the world, we know God has great plans for His two little girls, because He brought them through with few complications.

Today, our girls are growing into beautiful little girls and everyday our son is just a true amazement to us. So that is our family story. We thank God everyday for his protective watch over our kids, during the pregnancies and every day since. We have learned that even though we may not like the path our life is traveling at the moment, we trust God has a plan for us and if we just put our faith in Him; He will guide us through anything. To quote a friend of mine, "The road might be painful but His plans are always better for us in the long run!"

Katherine Guiles
Newark Valley, New York

~❧| Chapter 4 |❧~

The Miracle of the Three "H"s

November 2009 came, and armed with our video camera, we went to our first ultrasound appointment for this third pregnancy with hope and joy. We joked about what sex the baby would be, and told Channing what a great big brother he would make. However, as the ultrasound picture appeared on the screen, I knew right away that something was not right. It took the technician much too long to find the 10 week old baby, and the minute the image appeared on the screen, I knew it was over. The baby was much too small for 10 weeks, and later, I learned that the deformities that I saw were from the tiny body being re-absorbed into my system. There was no heartbeat on the screen, and of course, no movement from the miniature person in my womb. Kevin heard a heartbeat monitor in the room next door and told Channing to "listen," thinking it was our little one. It broke my heart. I knew that our little baby's heart was silent. The technician quietly told us that there was no heartbeat, and the baby was much too small. She left us to pull ourselves together before we saw the doctor, and I broke into tears. In a moment of sudden loss, we often know the truth, but rarely does it remove the pain and grief that we are feeling. Kevin tried to reassure me with all the right words, but right then, I just needed to cry.

After talking with the doctor, we made an appointment for a D&C (Dilation and Curettage/Suction Aspiration) for November 23rd, the day before my 31st birthday. It seemed so unfair. It seemed like we "deserved" something better. By this time, I had been pregnant for about four months and had had symptoms for about eight. I felt that it was all for nothing. We were back to square one again. Why was it that some women – especially those who were seemingly terrible moms – could just *think* the word "baby" and one landed in their lap? Why did *we* have to work so hard for this? The pain was real and it went deep into my heart and touched every aspect of my life.

There were three immediate issues that I needed to work through. I like to call them "the three h's." The first "h" that I dealt with was "hurt." It is so very painful to have to part with something precious to us, especially when it is a person. I had been writing letters to our little one from before we conceived, so I had grown attached to my precious baby, even before I had a chance to see him/her. Saying "good-bye" was very difficult, but something occurred to me: God was not asking me to give up anything that He had not given to me in the first place. He often asks us to sacrifice certain things in our lives - things which *He* has already given to us - back to Him. He uses those sacrifices to increase our faith and bring us closer to Himself. I think of the Bible stories of the feeding of the five thousand **[Matthew 14:13-21]**, and of the story of the widow and her son **[I Kings 17]**. In both stories, God asked for items that they already had in order to bless them. They had to have the faith to give up what they treasured, in order to see God's power at work. Sometimes, just like the widow, we are asked to give up the dearest and most precious thing in our lives, and often, God requires *all* of it, not just a portion. We entered this world with nothing, so anything and everything that we have is straight from the hand of our loving Heavenly Father.

Job 1:21 *- ...Naked came I out of my mother's womb, and naked shall I return thither: the LORD gave, and the LORD hath taken away; blessed be the name of the LORD.*

God has given me children, and so far, He has asked for two of them back. I may never understand every reason, but, once again, it is not for me to know the mind of God. I feel confident that His way is best, and that He will give me what I need, when I need it, and for whatever length of time I need it. The sovereignty and Lordship of God in our lives brings confidence during times of confusion and fear.

Another difficult part of hurting is what other people intentionally or unintentionally add to it. Regrettably, people do not always know exactly what to say or how to comfort people who are hurting. I found that I needed to prepare myself in advance to hear things that could potentially upset me, each and every time I told my story. I often heard things such as: "At least you already have a child," "You can always try again (as though another one would take the place of the one we lost)," "At least you can carry a child," "It must be God's will," "It just wasn't meant to be," "It could be worse...," "I know how you feel" (unless they also lost a child, they cannot possibly begin to understand how I am feeling),as well as many other ridiculous comments. I have had to learn to "read between the lines," and not let my spirit be crushed by a comment made with good intentions. If I put myself in another person's shoes (or even my own, before I had my first miscarriage), I understand that people truly have no idea what I am going through, nor could they. Most people merely want to be helpful and show their concern for me in a verbal way. It might not be completely appropriate, but I need to try to give them the benefit of the doubt. Also, I think that being prepared for thoughtless or empty conversations and keeping a positive attitude will certainly lessen the hurt that is added on by others. Maybe I need to be willing to tell people that, honestly, I just need them to be there, to listen, and sometimes, just to cry with me. I do not need a solution right now; I could simply use a "shoulder."

The second "h" that I faced was "helplessness." There is a positive and a negative side to this subject. On the negative side, I found myself, not only adopting a "why me?" mentality, but also comparing myself to others, and becoming quite bitter about the circumstance that I found myself in. It seems that there are so many moms out there who do not even *want* their children, and for some reason, they just keep right on having more. Why couldn't *they* have this difficulty instead of us? What about the unwed women, who practically prostitute themselves for "love," and wind up being mothers, without even thinking about it first, not to mention, planning or preparing for it? I consider myself to be a "good" mom, at least, for the most part. I try not to do anything to put my child in danger, I sacrifice almost daily for the welfare of my child, and I would even die to protect my child, if need be. Why do *I* deserve to lose a child? I knew that the solution to changing this mind-set was a very simple principle and was becoming a re-occurring theme in my walk with God. It was God's business, not mine. Period. He is God, and I am not. Comparing my situation to that of others, only allows the devil to steal my faith, joy, and contentment. I need to believe that if there were a better, easier, and more painless way for God to accomplish His will in my life, He would do it.

The positive side to this feeling of helplessness comes when we learn to let God truly have full reign in our hearts, minds, and lives. We truly have no power over the issues of life and death. The Bible says that there is very little that we can actually change. Sometimes, I find that faith is very elusive. I have to remind myself of the Biblical account of the man who admittedly had a lack of faith. He was not

ashamed to ask God for the faith that he needed for his son
to be healed.

*Mark 9: 23-24 - Jesus said to him, "If you can believe,
all things are possible to him who believes." Immediately
the father of the child cried out and said with tears,
"Lord, I believe; help my unbelief!"*

Jesus had compassion on this man and healed his child,
in spite of his lack of faith. I wonder if this was due to the
fact that the man had the humility to admit that he was inadequate in his own strength. I have also found the following
verse to be very helpful in my weakness as well:

*James 1:5 - "If any of you lack wisdom, let him ask of
God, who giveth to all men liberally..."*

What an incredible promise! What an encouragement
and comfort this should be to us in times of trials and tribulations. God has given us His Word and His Holy Spirit in
order to understand how we are to respond and how we can
find a way through the difficulties. His Word is so clear. As I
learn to draw upon the power of my wonderful and omnipotent Father, I find *my* helplessness to be completely trivial in
the light of *His* strength.

I have often found that when I am at my most helpless
moment, then, I am truly able to see God working in my
life. I have always been a creative and resourceful person.
If something needs to be done, I'll find a way. It is rare that
I cannot find what I need to accomplish a task or project.
Sometimes, this is more of a handicap than a gift. Often, I
find myself rushing to "fix" something that I really should
have prayed about first. My health concerns and the trials
that I face are often what I need to grow in my walk with
God. I usually need to get to the very "end" of myself, before

God can get a hold of my heart and life and make a change in me.

This leads into the last "h" – hope. One way to experience hope through my loss is by allowing God to be the LORD of my life. I have discovered that even though I know all of the right answers, unless I truly believe them with my head *and* my heart, those truths will never affect me or change the way I live. Not only do I need to *know* that God is sovereign and wants the very best for my life, I also need to *believe* it so fully that I let go of my own wants and desires and completely trust His plan for me. I do not think that this means that I will never experience fear, sadness, or disappointment, but I think that beneath those human emotions, I will sense the joy and peace that only God can give. If I can learn to replace the negative thoughts and feelings with positive ones, then, I truly believe that I will, eventually, make a habit of finding the good in every situation that I face. Already, I have noticed myself doing this more and more each passing day. This will bring lasting peace in my heart and mind.

> *Philippians 4:7-9* - *And the peace of God, which passeth all understanding, shall keep your hearts and minds through Christ Jesus. Finally, brethren, whatsoever things are true, whatsoever things are honest, whatsoever things are just, whatsoever things are pure, whatsoever things are lovely, whatsoever things are of good report; if there be any virtue, and if there be any praise, think on these things.*

Another source of hope is found in believing that I will meet my babies someday in heaven. I am so looking forward to learning if I had boys or girls, what they looked like, and how many I truly have. Of course, I have no idea what importance these things will have to me in heaven, but somehow, I feel that God will give us the answers for so many of the questions that we have now. I have heard many theories about whether or not babies go to heaven. I believe that scripture is very clear that God chose us before the foundation of the world, and that He has the authority to elect whomever He desires. It would take me chapters to explain how exactly I have come to the conclusion that my babies are in the presence of God right now. To keep it simple, I feel that the following passage helps to shed some light on this subject in the simplest of ways:

> *II Samuel 12:15-23 - And the LORD struck the child that Uriah's wife bore to David, and it became ill. David therefore pleaded with God for the child, and David fasted and went in and lay all night on the ground. So the elders of his house arose and went to him, to raise him up from the ground. But he would not, nor did he eat food with them. Then on the seventh day it came to pass that the child died. And the servants of David were afraid to tell him that the child was dead. For they said, "Indeed, while the child was alive, we spoke to him, and he would not heed our voice. How can we tell him that the child is dead? He may do some harm!" When David saw that his servants were whispering, David perceived that the child was dead. Therefore David said to his servants, "Is the child dead?"*
> *And they said, "He is dead." So David arose from the ground, washed and anointed himself, and changed his clothes; and he went into the house of the LORD and worshiped. Then he went to his own house; and when he requested, they set food before him, and he ate. Then his servants said to him, "What is this that you have done? You fasted and wept for the child while he was alive, but when the child died, you arose and ate food." And he said, "While the child was alive, I fasted and wept; for I said, 'Who can tell whether the LORD will be gracious*

to me, that the child may live?' But now he is dead; why should I fast? Can I bring him back again? I shall go to him, but he shall not return to me."

Even though David's child died as a consequence of David's sin, David still believed that He would "go to him" someday. Heaven holds the hope of closure on all of the pain and heartache that I will face in this lifetime. This truth keeps my focus upward, even in the darkest of times. I need to dwell on the positive, and not get "stuck" grieving the losses I have faced. Even David realized the futility in that. It is not always easy, but I cannot allow my mourning to interfere with God's will for my life. I have assurance that He will make everything "right" in the end.

When I step back and see the bigger picture, I actually feel that each trial I have faced has brought me closer to Christ-likeness. Even though the ultimate goal of perfection in Christ will not be complete, until I see Him face to face, it seems that every loss and every painful circumstance has made me stronger in faith and stronger in my compassion towards others. Often, we cannot show compassion or love, until it has been shown to us in the same degree. When we choose to allow God free reign in our lives, we will find a freedom and a security that is only found in His perfect plan.

John 8:32 - *And you shall know the truth, and the truth shall make you free.*

The following two testimonies are written by two very precious women, who God used in a special way to minister to me, after my second miscarriage. Each of them had a miscarriage around the same time that I had mine. We shared a special evening together exchanging heartaches, encouragement, and prayers for God's will and way to be accomplished in our lives. A little over a year later, God has blessed each of us with another baby - one to hold in our arms. These women will always have a special place in my heart and my healing.

I am writing my story over a year after my Angel Baby went to Heaven. Part of me wanted to write while the pain was still fresh, but it was just too difficult. Now, I have reflected over what happened, and am better able to see God's purpose through all of it.

My husband, Chad, and I already had a son, Elijah, who was three at the time we found out we were pregnant again. My parents were super excited for us, and just had to tell everyone. I wasn't very far along, and was just starting to tell people the good news. Seven weeks into my pregnancy, I started to spot. I didn't tell Chad at first, because I had no idea what was going on. The following day, I called my doctor's office and they asked me lots of questions. I finally told Chad. He told me to call the office back and ask to see my doctor. I made an appointment and had to have an ultrasound. That was one of the toughest days of my life, as the ultrasound confirmed what I had long suspected...a miscarriage. I was told to go back into the waiting room, and my doctor would see us in a while in his office. Waiting in that room full of pregnant women made me so angry. I was angry with them for being able to carry their babies. Why couldn't I?

My doctor is wonderful, and I couldn't ask for someone so compassionate and kind. He told us that he thought it would be best to "let nature take its course," and try to avoid having a D&C. I remember that day, when I saw my Angel Baby for the first time. It was a horrible, horrible moment, and an image that will never escape my mind. I loved him/her, from the moment I realized I was pregnant. I will always love my little Angel Baby, and will see him/her one day when I part this earth.

I truly believe that women cannot fully understand about miscarriage, unless having gone through it themselves. I do not wish it upon anyone. My friend, Holly, had lost two precious children to miscarriage, and my friend, Michelle, had just lost her baby after seven weeks - about a month before myself. Now, I realized what they were going through. We looked to each other and found comfort. There was another story that gave me strength and comfort. That was the story of Angie Smith and her husband, Todd, who is the lead singer for the Christian group "Selah." I read her book "I Will Carry You," and it gave me the peace that I needed to get through this difficult time. I bought the sheet music for "I Will Carry You (Audrey's Song)." The song made me feel sad and happy at the same time. I was sad that I would never be able to take my child's picture or watch him/her grow up. However, there was happiness in my heart, because the Lord could show him/her far more than I ever could.

It's sometimes amazing what God can make come out of trials. A little over a year later, I was blessed with another beautiful baby boy, Levi. My friends Holly and Michelle were also each blessed with another child. There are still times when I weep for my Angel Baby, but the pain is less now. The Lord brought me through this difficult time, because I leaned on Him to guide me and bring me strength. My intention for writing this is just to let others know to look to the Lord in these tough times, because He will be there for you always.

Philippians 4:13 - *"I can do all things through Christ which strengtheneth me.*

Mary

The experience as a whole would have been more tolerable if my husband were able to be by my side during the entire day; from driving to the ER first thing in the morning right until I was able to walk out of the doctor's office with the D&C complete. If he were with me, he would know how scared and alone I was, going through triage and having to explain to every nurse, physician, and attendant why I was there. I eventually became numb to saying, "I'm 7 weeks pregnant, and I'm bleeding." He would have understood the perception I had of the ER physician on duty, and why I refused him performing any kind of internal exam, because I didn't feel comfortable with his cocky attitude. He would know a little better how to comfort me, after experiencing the sights and sounds of a D&C at the doctor's office later that day.

No, this is not my husband's fault, nor am I blaming any of this procedure on him. I just think that I would have had an easier time that day, if I had had his support in person, rather than a few phone calls and text messages. It is in fact my fault that he wasn't there. I could have told him that I needed him next to me, rather than have him at work. I didn't know just how badly I needed him.

From the very beginning, I had a feeling that this pregnancy was not "right". At the time that I took the at-home test, I was experiencing, what I thought, was a really bad flu. After a positive confirmation, we decided to nickname the new baby "Baby Hercules" or "Baby H" for short, because of the extreme illness we thought he was imposing on my body. In a couple of days, my husband became sick with the flu – the same exact symptoms I had. Okay, so I had both the flu and was pregnant, but not experiencing any morning sickness (after this flu bout passed). I didn't even have the "feeling" that I was pregnant. I had had the "feeling" with my other 2 pregnancies: slightly tender breasts and a little queasiness.

After about a week of still not feeling pregnant, I took another home test just to confirm. Positive again. I didn't understand how I could feel absolutely fine and still be pregnant. Should I consider myself lucky or was something not right?

We only told a couple of friends about this new pregnancy, until I had an OB visit and ultrasound. The first ultrasound measured Baby H at 6 weeks. I could see the heartbeat on the screen and little movements. What a relief! There really was a baby, and it seemed to be okay.

We started to tell more friends and family members, even though I kept mentioning that, "I still don't 'feel' pregnant." I bought a few summer maternity tops, and was starting to get a little more excited. My husband and I spent an afternoon looking at mini vans and bunk beds, in anticipation of the new arrival, several months down the road.

Exactly a week after that ultrasound, I woke up with a little bleeding. I was advised by my doctor's office to head straight to the emergency room. My husband left for work. I took our older two children to my mom's, and went straight to the ER. The parking lot security guard had stopped me before letting me into the ER lot, "Are you here for an emergency?" he asked. "Yes," I replied. "Are you here to see someone, or are you here for yourself?" he asked trying to determine my necessity for parking in the reserved lot. Choking back tears, I said, "myself". I could sense him watching me as I parked my car and walked to the building. *He probably thinks I'm lying just to get a good parking spot.*

I had a difficult time composing myself in triage and getting settled into my room. Eventually, I was wheeled down for an ultrasound. Before the lights were dimmed, the technician had informed me that she couldn't let me see the screen or give me any information on the status of the pregnancy, because of specific emergency room procedures that needed to be followed. Once she started, I could tell by her stone-cold demeanor that something was not right. I had to wait about another 2 hours for the attending physician to come in to give me the results. Seemingly, without any concern, he blurted out that, "there isn't any heartbeat and the fetus is measuring at 5 weeks," but he still wanted to do an internal exam. That's when I replied, "No, I'd rather just go home, or go see my own doctor".

I have come to the conclusion that when expecting to be admitted to the ER, be prepared for a LOT of waiting - waiting for tests, waiting for the results, waiting over an hour for discharge papers…waiting and wondering. A good time to be praying. By this point I knew that our "Baby H" had gone to heaven, and would be waiting there to meet with us someday. How joyful it will be to one day hold this sweet little baby.

After spending over 5 long and agonizing hours in the ER, I drove straight to my doctor's office, where I was immediately treated with respect and comforted by my doctor and the members of his staff. I was given a few choices: have a D&C that day in his office, have a D&C the next day in his office, have a D&C scheduled at the hospital in the next week, or let the miscarriage complete itself naturally. I looked at him and said, "I don't know. I really just don't know." I didn't know what to do. I tried calling my husband, who was working in a secure area at work where cell phones weren't permitted. I couldn't get through. I had to make this decision on my own. I had no idea what to do. A few of the staff members told me about their own personal experiences with miscarriages and the decisions that they made at this point. I decided to go through with the D&C that same day, even though I would be limited as to how much pain control I would be administered, because I did have to drive home after it was complete.

The staff at my doctor's office was absolutely amazing with trying to make me as comfortable as possible; from playing soft music in the room, to actually holding my hands and rubbing my shoulder during the entire procedure. It was not a pleasant experience, that's for sure. It was quite painful. Every single part of it was in one way painful, uncomfortable, or *weird*. I have never had a D&C performed, and I didn't really know what one was, let alone, what to expect.

I am still in the healing process, both physically and emotionally. Physically, I feel fine, just a little spotting, since it has only been 3 days since my miscarriage. I didn't have any cramping, excessive bleeding, or any other complications, thankfully. Every now and then, I have a "sad moment" - not as often today as the day after the procedure. There have been some tears related to grieving, but probably more due to crazed hormones, and just that my husband can't share in my feelings. This will pass, but I'm sure there will be some events down the road that will trigger some more emotions.

Through this experience I can see God's perfect timing and his perfect planning. He chose the day I was going to start bleeding, and it was perfect. If it were the day before, I would have been at work the whole day. If it were the day after, we were scheduling a trip out of town early that morning.

Psalm 18:30 - "As for God, His way is perfect..."

I often wonder why this happened to me, to my baby. I have to remind myself that God does have a purpose for everything and everything happens for a reason. He creates everything for his glory [**Isaiah 43:7**], and that includes our "Baby H".

I will never take another pregnancy for granted. When my husband and I decide to try again, and if God does give us another chance at being pregnant, I'm hoping that my thankfulness will overshadow the fear of losing another baby.

Michelle

-⊰❦⊹ Chapter 5 ⊹❦⊱-

The Miracle of Conquering Adversity

After the loss of our second baby, we were somewhat surprised at where the majority of our subsequent challenges originated from. I had thought that dealing with the death of our child would be one of the greatest difficulties that we could ever face. Unfortunately and surprisingly, even bigger challenges were found in the places that were least expected. Of course, some of these complications were completely predictable, though not always as easy to deal with as I might have guessed they would have been. I feel that there were three major areas from which these challenges, which were essential for me to learn to conquer adversity *God's* way, came from. I still find myself needing to be reminded, frequently, of the truths that I discovered during this time.

The first place that I found adversity was within my own self. It came in the form of the need for healing – physical, emotional, and spiritual healing. First of all, I had my physical healing to deal with. This D&C was the first surgery that I had ever had, and it seems as though this must be one of the most basic surgeries to have and to heal from; however, recovering from a *pregnancy* – no matter how short or long it was – is still a challenge. I had all of the ordinary issues following a birth, such as: bleeding, cramping, pain, and the hormonal "roller-coaster ride." It was a lot more difficult to deal with these typically "minor issues," when there wasn't a baby, the usual "major issue," to keep my mind occupied. I had always felt that the true beauty of pregnancy, labor, and delivery is taking your little one home to cuddle and care for when it is all said and done. My arms were empty, my heart was broken, and I certainly could not see anything "beautiful" in this situation.

This emptiness and brokenness that I felt contributed to the second type of healing – emotional. The loss of a child was hard enough, but then, having to deal with a procedure - one that thousands of women choose every year in order to *knowingly* end their pregnancies - just made it that much harder. Of the nearly 1.5 million abortions that are performed each year, almost 90% of them occur before 12 weeks and can be done with a D&C procedure. Just the knowledge of that broke my heart all over again. The fear of allowing someone to just "tear" your child from your womb, in such an undignified way, was so real and so painful to me. As I lay in the room, waiting for the doctor, I just wanted to scream, "NO! Don't do this to me! Please, don't take my baby! I want to keep him!" Of course, I knew that this baby could never go home with me, and that our little one was already in a heavenly home, but my child was a piece of me. I did not know how attached I had already become, until that very moment. It was kind of ironic how this became so real to me, just before I had to let go. Sometimes, it really does take losing something to realize what you had to begin with. Going home after this procedure was very draining. I walked into the hospital pregnant, and walked out "not." The night after the ultrasound, I wrote the following letter to my heavenly child:

Our Dear Little Baby Brooks,

You have left my life as quickly as you came. I will never hold you, though I saw you once - so small, so perfect, yet incomplete. Your little heart beat below mine, only for a short while, but the "sound" it made in my life will last forever. I'll never touch your little toes or caress your soft sweet cheek. I'll never have the chance to grasp your precious hand or feel your fingers on my face. But as my tears come falling down, I paint myself this picture... I see the face of Jesus as He gazes at His lap, and in His arms He holds you tight and softly says your name. My Baby, you are safe now – as safe as you can be, resting in the nail-scared hands of the Christ of Calvary.

I look forward to meeting you someday. Until then, I pray that Jesus will tell you about us and how much we love you, since we will never have the privilege of telling you about Him. I knew the moment that I saw you, that something wasn't right. But in the end, I understand that everything IS right after all. It is just how God wants it to be. You opened your beautiful eyes for the first time to behold your Savior and Lord. You are in the very best place possible, and we will hold you always in our hearts. I feel honored that He allowed me to carry you, even for a short while. What a blessing to have a baby just for Him. You were a rare gift – so close, and yet, at the same time, so very far away from my arms. We will never forget you.

We love you, Little One. Rest in the arms of Jesus...

Your loving Parents

II Samuel 12:22-23

(Written with love for and in memory of our precious little Brooks Frieden (German for "peace")Besser, who passed away in November of 2009.)

Lastly, and most importantly, was the spiritual healing. I felt discouraged and guilty. Discouragement went to work with fury, and once again, I wondered why being pregnant was so easy for some people, but so very hard for me. I remember telling my sister, when I was in high school, that I had a "feeling" that I would lose a child someday. The "feeling" was always in the back of my mind, but I always dismissed it. I never knew why I felt that way, and I guess I figured that it was just some silly immature way of feeling closer to the will of God. Maybe, God was trying to prepare my heart. The day that I walked out of that ultrasound, I said, to myself, "I knew it!" I did not tell anyone about this at the time, but somehow I felt like it was some sort of "prophecy" being fulfilled in my life. I never blamed God or got angry with Him, during this difficult time of loss. Long ago, I learned how to overcome this temptation in my heart. I often think of the story of Jacob when he wrestled with God:

Genesis 32: 24-32 - And Jacob was left alone; and there wrestled a man with him until the breaking of the day. And when he saw that he prevailed not against him, he touched the hollow of his thigh; and the hollow of Jacob's thigh was out of joint, as he wrestled with him. And he said, Let me go, for the day breaketh. And he said, I will not let thee go, except thou bless me. And he said unto him, What is thy name? And he said, Jacob. And he said, Thy name shall be called no more Jacob, but Israel: for as a prince hast thou power with God and with men, and hast prevailed. And Jacob asked him, and said, Tell me, I pray thee, thy name. And he said, Wherefore is it that thou dost ask after my name? And he blessed him there. And Jacob called the name of the place Peniel: for I have seen God face to face, and my life is preserved. And as he passed over Penuel the sun rose upon him, and he halted upon his thigh. Therefore the children of Israel eat not of the sinew which shrank, which is upon the hollow of the thigh, unto this day: because he touched the hollow of Jacob's thigh in the sinew that shrank.

Even though Jacob limped for the remainder of his life, he had glimpsed the face of God, and his life and his identity were changed forever. My God might not make complete sense to me all of the time, but who am I to question the mind of God? Why should I not believe that He is the same God *now*, as He was when I became pregnant? It does not make any sense to trust Him in the good times, and then, blame Him in the bad times. If I cannot trust Him with these "small" things, how can I possibly trust Him with my eternal security? I may have a new "limp" in my soul, but I have certainly seen the Almighty at work in my life through this pain, and I will definitely never be the same again.

Guilt...what another heavy burden to bear! Even during the post-op visit with my doctor, my mind raced to think of anything that I might have done to harm this innocent and helpless child. My *only* "job," in regards to this unborn child, was to be a safe place for my baby to develop and grow for nine months. How had I managed to fail at this one "small" task? Too much medication? The wrong diet? Stress? I came up with a countless number of things that I may have somehow done "wrong," and the guilt began to weigh heavy on me. I knew that I needed to deal with this problem right away, before it destroyed me. I had certainly witnessed what guilt could do if it was left to run amuck. I needed to stop my worrying, and face the facts:

Psalm 46:10a - *Be still, and know that I am God...*

Psalm 100:3 - *Know ye that the LORD he is God: it is he that hath made us, and not we ourselves; we are his people, and the sheep of his pasture.*

1 Peter 5:7 - *Casting all your care upon him; for he careth for you.*

Philippians 2:13 - *For it is God which worketh in you both to will and to do of his good pleasure.*

Proverbs 16:9 - *A man's heart deviseth his way: but the LORD directeth his steps.*

I was putting my God in a very small box, and limiting who He is and what He is able to do. Somehow, I felt that I was capable of doing something that God could not undo or prevent. What a terrible lie! My Heavenly Father is so much bigger than I am or anything I could ever choose to do. He could surely "supersede" anything harmful that I did, either deliberately or inadvertently. Occasionally, the devil tries to deceive me into taking this burden back upon myself, but when I consider the truth about my God, I can refuse with clarity and resolve.

Not only did I feel that, somehow, I must have done something to cause my child's untimely death, but I also felt that I was somehow "unholy" or lacked faith, because of the pain and fear that I felt afterwards. If I verbalized these feelings I had, other people might think that I did not trust God, or that I needed to read my Bible or pray more. I began some serious soul-searching at this point. I needed to make sure that my strength was coming from God and not from myself. In my search, I became convinced that "grieving" is a natural human emotion, common to believers and non-believers alike. However, I also determined that because I have the hope of meeting my child in heaven one day and because I serve an omniscient God, my grieving should not be like that of non-believers, who have no hope.

1 Thessalonians 4:13 - *But I would not have you to be ignorant, brethren, concerning them which are asleep, that ye sorrow not, even as others which have no hope.*

Another issue in my life, "fear," was much more difficult of a problem. I was not dealing with a phobia, by any means. It was just that nagging fear that lurked in the back of my mind at the thought of another pregnancy. However, it seemed that God sent just the right people in my path to give me guidance, counsel, and encouragement. I came to a personal conclusion that fear and trust can go hand in hand. I think there is a difference between "fear which controls *you*" and "fear that *you* control." *Controlled* fear is healthy. It keeps us safe and alert. It is what you do with that fear that determines your faith in God. I prayed about gaining control over my fear, often, during this time in my life. If I allowed my fear to get in the way of how I should be living before God, or allowed it to hinder my testimony before others, then, it would be sin. I certainly had no desire to even start down a path of destructive grief or fear.

John 14:27 - *Peace I leave with you, my peace I give unto you: not as the world giveth, give I unto you. Let not your heart be troubled, neither let it be afraid.*

Psalm 56:3 - *What time I am afraid, I will trust in thee.*

Finding victory over the challenges in my own self was, and sometimes still is, truly a battle. I needed to understand that I could not just "get over it" or "move on" when dealing with the loss of my little ones, no matter what anyone else said or thought. I had to learn a new way of living that included the memories and the blessings that *are* those children. *I* will be the only mom that my babies will ever have, and learning to embrace that thought, brought happiness back into my life. God's main purpose for those children was to bring glory to Himself. If there are other reasons, I may never know. However, I knew that I had to find a way to share God's glory through my loss. God's grace is truly sufficient, even when it does not feel like it.

2 Corinthians 12:9 - And he said unto me, My grace is sufficient for thee: for my strength is made perfect in weakness. Most gladly therefore will I rather glory in my infirmities, that the power of Christ may rest upon me.

The second major adversity that I needed to claim victory over was other people's "involvement" in my situation. During this experience, I watched my MOPS (Mothers of Preschoolers) group - women I had only met one time before our loss - immediately jump at the opportunity to bless us. They provided meals for almost two weeks, in order to get us through to Thanksgiving. We were so very touched. I did not have words to describe how my heart felt. God used these people, who we hardly even knew, in an amazing way, to make our lives a little easier during an emotional time. On the other hand, we were saddened and disappointed in the people and places that we discovered a lack of support. Those, who could have easily sympathized with our pain, chose to disregard it instead. It seemed so backwards. *My heart could not help but ache for other women, who had faced or would face this same sorrow in their lives.*

We were also shocked that our church, at the time, did not reach out to us. A few people within the church reached out to us, but the pastor actually waited two weeks before calling to offer any support. The places where we would have expected the most prayer, support, and love to come from, had left us empty. It was easy to let myself feel "wronged," and I was tempted to throw myself a gigantic pity-party. However, I soon found that the best thing that I could do was to try to "expect the unexpected" – good and bad. I was learning that most of my anger stemmed from my expectations not being met. I need to learn to not have expectations, which I cannot control, for others. I must look only to *God* to meet my needs for comfort and love. I think that we often use the word "obligation" very loosely and expect those in our life to use it the same way.

Unfortunately, most of us are self-centered a large extent of the time, and we often fail to see those who are in need and in pain around us. This was certainly an eye-opening experience for me. I need to look for opportunities to show compassion to people who are suffering, even when it is not *convenient* for me to do so. We show that we are Christians by our love. Once again, my testimony was at stake.

John 13:35 - By this shall all men know that ye are my disciples, if ye have love one to another.

Another way to deal with outside influence on a situation is to decide in advance what kind of involvement I want and from whom. When I left the doctor's office that day, only Kevin and I knew what had happened. I had a choice of whom to tell and what to tell them. Of course, some people will find out due to simple gossip, but for the most part, I know who I can trust and who I cannot. This was certainly a learning time, as I really did not even consider telling one person and not another. I regard myself as an outgoing and social person. I needed the encouragement and support of others, even if that meant that I needed to overlook or just ignore some comments or maybe, a lack of interest on some people's part. The "good" completely outweighed the "bad" for me. For the most part, people cannot deal well with difficult circumstances without the help of *other* people. *God* is certainly our first and most significant help in time of need, but He gave us spouses, family, friends, and acquaintances for a reason. Even Adam, in the Garden of Eden, was lacking, without a help-meet. The need for human companionship was created within us. I thank God for reaching out to us in a physical way that we can understand, and that we can find comfort in. I just need to remember not to expect from *people* what only *God* can provide.

Lastly, but most problematical, was the victory that I needed, and still need, to find over the devil each day. We are told that the adversary of our soul is fierce and treacherous:

> *1 Peter 5:8 - Be sober, be vigilant; because your adversary the devil, as a roaring lion, walketh about, seeking whom he may devour.*

There is no doubt that the devil looks for and delights in these difficult trials in our lives. He desires to destroy those who would suffer with distinction and seek to bring glory to God through those sufferings. Our weakness can either be the devil's advantage or God's opportunity. This sounds like a relatively simple choice, but it definitely takes continuous steadfastness and faith to maintain our resolve. The Bible tells us how to avoid falling into the enemy's snares:

> *James 4:7 - Submit yourselves therefore to God. Resist the devil, and he will flee from you.*

I also need to prepare in advance for the trials that *will* come. As Christians, God tells us to expect trials and tribulations in this world, so we should not be surprised by them.

> *John 16:33 - These things I have spoken unto you, that in me ye might have peace. In the world ye shall have tribulation: but be of good cheer; I have overcome the world.*

II Corinthians 4:8-9 - *We are troubled on every side, yet not distressed; we are perplexed, but not in despair; Persecuted, but not forsaken; cast down, but not destroyed.*

I used to ask, "Why me?" but now I ask, "Why *not* me?" Spiritual warfare is very real, and I find this to be true more and more each day. It should never come as a surprise that the devil would try to use my weaknesses to conquer me. We certainly do not want to live our life by a "what if" philosophy. Allowing ourselves to question *everything* just makes us pessimists and worriers. However, on the other hand, being prepared for what *could* happen (sometimes by putting ourselves in other people's shoes) can be truly helpful. Not only can we try to identify with others better, but we can also make sure that our attitudes and our hearts are focused on God, and *His* will for our lives. We need to be prepared to accept *whatever* God has planned.

Philippians 3:13-14 - *Brethren, I count not myself to have apprehended: but this one thing I do, forgetting those things which are behind, and reaching forth unto those things which are before. I press toward the mark for the prize of the high calling of God in Christ Jesus.*

Finding victory in these areas is easier said than done. I find that I need to work this out each time I go through a difficult circumstance, especially one that lends itself to the critiques of others. Learning to control *myself* is certainly a daily task, and it takes the strength and wisdom of God.

1 Corinthians 9:27 - *But I keep under my body, and bring it into subjection: lest that by any means, when I have preached to others, I myself should be a castaway.*

Once again, I find that dwelling on "…whatsoever things are honest, …just, …lovely, and…are of good report…" will eventually replace the negativity and discouragement in my heart and bring me "the peace of God, which passeth all understanding…" [*Philippians 4:7-9*] My God is God in the good times, and He is still God in the bad times. He never changes. He never fails. I now know that God cannot fill my heart, if it is already full of bitterness, anger, and negative thinking.

James 1:17 - *Every good gift and every perfect gift is from above, and cometh down from the Father of lights, with whom is no variableness, neither shadow of turning.*

My husband and I were in a marital crisis. "Crisis" is a kind word for how bad it really was, at the time. I had actually used the word "divorce" a few times, in my rawest moments, and many nights were spent in separate rooms. As a result, intimacy had been rare in the year leading up to July 13, 2009. We came together once in April and once in May, according to my journal. Pregnancy never even crossed my mind. Why would it? I had Luteal Phase Defect and he had low motility and count. We already had our miracle child, and I was hardly expecting another one, given our history plus our circumstances.

Early June, I began feeling like I was pregnant, but like every other woman with infertility, told myself not to be stupid and confuse period symptoms with pregnancy symptoms. I also sternly told myself that there would be no HPT sticks getting peed on, until I was a month overdue. One can handle only so many negatives, and with time, you steel your heart against, yet another, "one-liner" and don't allow yourself to test, until you can be guaranteed a two-line result.

No matter how stern my inner monologue was; however, one day, I caved and did test. BFN, or "big fat negative," as it's known on infertility forums. I threw the test away, and stepped in the shower. My shower finished, I dug into the trash just to make sure it was definitely negative. That's when I saw the second line. I remember staring at it for several minutes. Then, I told myself that it had been more than 10 minutes, so I was seeing an evaporation line and to let it go.

During the time that I began feeling pregnant, a pain began in my right lower abdomen. It was - what I thought at the time - the all-too-familiar pain of an ovarian cyst. *"This is the reason for feeling pregnant,"* were my thoughts. *"You've had these mock-pregnancy symptoms before (nausea, late period), and my body is being cruel and doing it again."*

June 14th, my period came - heavy, painful, and as heartbreaking as always. Even when you're not "trying" and everything seems to be against getting pregnant, you still hold onto a vague hope. A hope you don't even realize you had, until you see red. Still, even with my period, the abdominal pain stayed, even after the cramps faded away. That was unusual. Usually cysts brought pain surrounding my period, but I could find relief after it ended. Ironically, the pain grew so intense that I would dream at night that I was in labor and giving birth. I even joked with my OB, when I saw her at church, about dreaming of her helping me deliver a baby boy. If I only had known…

The feeling of tender breasts began, reminiscent of pregnancy. I was aware of it, but told myself that because I had had my period, testing was a moot point. The pregnancy test had shown nothing but an evaporation line. End of story. Then, the bloating began. My tummy began to swell. No matter how much pilates and yoga I did, and despite my in-law's scales telling me that I was actually *losing* weight, my tummy grew. All through June, it became larger and harder, especially on the right side. It was a weird type of growth—a bloated look with hardness. *"That cyst is really going to give me a run for my money,"* was my thought.

The first week of July came, and the pain grew worse. At times, I would let myself linger on the thought of pregnancy and would even have a "knowing" feeling that I was, but then, I would think, *"But I had a period June 14th. I can't be pregnant! I saw that line after 20 minutes so it was an evaporation line. Both things pointed towards NOT being pregnant. Just stop with the wild imagination already!"*

Wednesday, July 8th, Chuck came home to find me hunched over the counter, as I fixed supper. When he asked what was wrong, I said that I either had a really bad case of Irritable Bowel Syndrome, a result of my former eating-disorder days – which really made no sense, because my diet is designed to prevent those flare-ups, or I had an ovarian cyst that was growing really big. He asked if I needed to go somewhere or call my GYN. I said, "No, I don't want to look like a fool if nothing is wrong". I was more frightened by the thought of looking like a hypochondriac wanting attention than I was by the pain.

Still, the pain nagged at me, and my concern grew. Thursday... Friday... Saturday... Sunday... I gardened, we had family over for dinner and dessert, and we even made love once again, for the first time in almost 6 weeks. I went to church on Sunday. I discipled a young woman on Monday morning, who ironically asked me to attend the birth of her second child, one that she felt "absolutely no excitement or love for." All the while, the pain was growing more and more intense.

On Monday afternoon, July 13th, I put Miracle down for her nap, went to my computer desk to begin my afternoon's work, and hit the floor. The pain took my breath away, and I thought I was going to pass out. The thought frightened me. My husband's summer work days usually lasted until sunset, and the thought of being unconscious, while my 1 ½ year old daughter cried for me from her crib, until Chuck got home that night, had me fighting to stay conscious, through the haze of pain. I crawled to my phone and called my husband at work. I didn't *ask*, I *told* him that he needed to come home immediately! I then called my Gynecologist, but hung up when I got her voice mail. I still felt foolish, and I didn't want to bother her unnecessarily.

Instantly after I hung up the phone, the knowledge slammed my heart, *"I'm pregnant, it's a tubal, and it's bad"*. As I was rocking on my hands and knees on the floor, I called my doctor's office again. This time, I left a voice mail and told her that something was very wrong, and that I thought it was gynecological-related. Her nurse called me back right away.

"Melissa, are you pregnant?"

"I don't know. I had a period in June...but I've been feeling pregnant. I just don't know. I just know something is wrong."

She asked me to describe my pain again. When I mentioned that the pain was shooting down my leg and up into my shoulder, a serious tone came into her voice. She told me to stay on the line. By that point, Chuck was home, and we were in the truck headed to the ER. My cell lost reception on the way to the hospital, and as I was signing into the ER, she called back. "Don't sign into the ER!" the nurse told me. "Instead, go a block over to the lab and then to radiology. We are by-passing the ER and going straight to testing."

I will never figure out how I was able to walk from the ER to the next block and into the hospital lab. I got into the lab, saw a full waiting room and a sign that said I had to register across the hall, and almost lost it then and there. Going to the desk, I almost passed out, but managed to explain that my Gynecologist had sent me in. How grateful I am that the woman at the desk believed that I was in pain, and she took me out back immediately, so people didn't stare. I'm not sure how long we waited, but it felt like a life-time. The pain was consuming me. My blood was drawn, and I went on my way to radiology. The women behind the desk treated me like I was a nuisance, and snidely told me to drink water for my ultrasound. I waited 45 minutes to get my ultrasound, and I couldn't handle the full bladder on top of the abdominal pain. The women acted appalled that I used the bathroom, but I just could not deal with the bladder pain. I kept seeing "spots," but kept willing myself to stay conscious for the sake of my daughter.

I was finally called to the ultrasound room. The tech's face was unreadable. My pain was unbearable. She sent me back into the waiting room. Another lifetime passed. I wanted so badly to lie down, but I forced myself to sit up, elbows on my knees, breathing through pain that, at that point was sharper than my labor, with Miracle, had been. Labor was intense, without drugs, but this was a different type of pain that radiated into my shoulders and down my legs.

The tech came back and asked me to go back to the ultrasound room. On the way she told me that Dr. Miller was on the phone. *"Dr Miller?"* I wondered. *"She's only my doctor if I'm pregnant. I see her FNP for all my gyne-cological needs. Why isn't Karen in on this any longer?"* Once in the ultrasound room, the tech handed me the phone. There, our "beloved Dr. Carol", as we call her, came over the line, "Melissa, you're in a lot of pain aren't you?" Me, ever fearing being a hypochondriac and looking like a fool if I said "yes," when nothing was wrong, replied, "I think it's better now." She came back with, "No it's not. You have a ruptured ectopic pregnancy. Your belly is full of blood. You are in a life-threatening situation. We need to get you into surgery immediately." Within a matter of a few seconds, the gift I longed for was handed to me and snatched from me. Do you remember the show "Touched by an Angel," where the angels revealed themselves at the end of the show, and everything around them and the main character went into freeze frame? That's what happened to me. My world stopped. My mind was processing, *"Pregnant. . .baby is gone. . . belly full of blood. . . life-threatening situation. . . your life is on the line."*

The tech, just a young girl, looked white and appeared as though she might cry. She had to go find a wheelchair, and as she left the room, I told Chuck what Dr. Carol had said. Then, I looked at Miracle, and I lost it. I picked her up and kissed her over and over again. I began begging Chuck to make sure that she grew up knowing that I loved her with all my heart, and to make sure he gave her the journal, in which I had written letters to her. I just kept saying, "I'm not ready to leave her. I don't want her to grow up without a Mama. Oh God, please let me stay here with my girl. She'll be so sad without me. Oh God, let me live."

Chuck began crying and then we started making phone calls. My best friend in Texas was my first call, and then, my inner circle of friends. No one answered. I was frantically going through my phone trying to get *anyone* on the phone. Although it was no one's fault, no one picked up. My only thought was, *"I need people to pray, if my life is indeed on the line. I need them to pray I stay here for my Miracle girl."*

The pain receded a bit in those moments, as all I had focused on loving Miracle. I grabbed her face in my hands, looked her in the eyes, and told her how much I loved her. All the while, willing her 20 month old mind to take a snapshot of her Mama telling her that, in case it was the last time she heard it from me.

The tech was back, still white as a ghost (funny how that sticks out in my mind), and next thing I know, I was being wheeled down halls, into an elevator, and then, into a room. The first person I saw was my favorite nurse, from when my daughter was born. She remembered us and had just recently transferred from labor and delivery to the surgical unit. Two pivotal points in my life with the same exact nurse. What are the chances? Everything blurred at that point, as the pain came back. They tried to put an IV in and blew two veins.

On the third attempt, I almost passed out - - me, the one who watches them take my blood and give me shots, couldn't deal with the pain of the needle because of the pain in my abdomen. For the first time that day, I finally got to lie down. People were "swarming" me. Asking me question upon question, from a list of my possessions to medical history and even asking me to sign an organ-donor form. Someone from the lab came and took more blood.

And Miracle was there through it all, along with my husband's teary face.

I was hit with Fentanyl, which cut the pain, but despite the haze of this medicine, I went into super logic mode, writing lists of where Mira's clothes and PJ's were, her favorite blankie and teddy bear, and people that needed to be called like my brother and our Pastor, etc.

Then, there was the warm, comforting face of Dr Carol's coming into the pre-op room. I fell apart, as I looked at her and said, "I wanted this baby so bad". She responded with, "I know...but right now I'm focused on you, Melissa." Her seriousness stopped my tears, and I pulled it together once again as she too, asked me questions to prep for surgery. The pain began to come back, as they wheeled me into the "holding area." At that point, I was alone. I'm sure it wasn't a long wait before surgery, but it hung in time for me. During that time, lying there, alone, I can remember thinking, *"I'm so glad Chuck and I came together yesterday, after all our time apart. So glad he has that to remember."* In that moment, knowing my life was at risk, I thought of all that God and I have been through these many years and laid there knowing that, really, I had no regrets. The only regrets that I had were not praying for my husband, during all the past months of hurt, but instead, harboring resentment against him and blocking him out of my heart. I was heartbroken over wondering if Miracle would grow up without a Mama, and I remember thinking that I wished I had interceded for people more and trusted God more concerning my marriage. Besides those few things, I had a sense of peace about my life - a wonderful, beautiful sense of peace.

Finally, in those moments alone, I talked to the baby, even though I knew he/she was dead. Those moments, as we waited for Dr. Carol to get ready for my surgery, were all I had in this relationship with my baby. In a matter of time, he or she would be removed from my body. In some ways, I still had him or her with me. So I laid there and silently told him/her how much he/she was wanted, how much we would grieve, how sorry I was that I hadn't known he/she was with me, and how I couldn't wait to see him/her in heaven some day.

Soon, I was being wheeled to the OR, and Dr. Carol was right there with us as we went. They were teasing me about my lunch that day—a spinach/Swiss chard smoothie with apples, oranges, and a banana and I remember Dr Carol saying, "A girl after my own heart" and someone saying, "You eat that way too Dr. Miller?!" I remember saying, "Oh, but I still like my Starbucks" in the same breath that I said, "That burns horribly," as they put the anesthesia in my IV. I remember hearing, "You won't feel it in another minute," and Dr. Miller's laughter somewhere in the background as she said, "I still like my Starbuck's too!" Then, the pain, after all those weeks, was temporarily gone as I fell asleep.

When they woke me up in recovery, I asked them not to. I remember telling them to just let me sleep. It hurt so bad. I kept coming in and out but remember coming into clarity, when they told me I was being taken to the maternity wing. I begged them not to do that to me. Turns out, there was a fire there earlier that day, so I went another floor. Once in recovery, Chuck told me Dr. Carol couldn't save my fallopian tube. She would later tell us that it was "shredded," and the situation had, indeed, been very serious and life-threatening. The haze of pain and drugs came and went for the next 12 hours. I wanted the catheter out, but I was thankful for it, because it hurt much too badly to walk to the bathroom. I'd wake up, remember the baby and Miracle, and fall back into sleep again - an endless cycle of pain all that night. Then, the post-op nausea kicked in. Insult to injury.

They take care of you medically, but no one is there for you emotionally and mentally in the hours and days after your experience. Because I wasn't on the maternity wing, I had nurses that had no clue what to say to me. I can't tell you how many told me about women with "just one working side and all the kids they had". I wanted to scream. They were probably trying to give me hope. To me, they were invalidating the pain of losing my tube and my baby.

My two days in the hospital I wanted to do nothing but take pain meds, curl up into a little ball and sleep. I didn't want to eat, I didn't want to talk, and I certainly didn't want to walk around, trying to get over the stiffness. But prior life experience has taught me that the longer you lay in bed and let the darkness take you, the harder it is to get out of it. So, I forced myself to eat, to get up and walk, to shower, or even to put on some makeup. Dr. Carol commented on what a strong woman I was. I may have looked strong, but truth was, I was dying inside. When I was up walking, I wanted to be in bed sleeping. When I was eating, I wanted to starve to death. When I carried on a normal conversation, I wanted to cry.

They don't tell you what to expect. No nurses told me I would begin bleeding badly. I didn't while in the hospital - I just spotted, but that's all. Friday, at home, the cramping - horrible, terrible cramping - and bleeding began. This frightened me. After all, I had almost waited too long with the abdominal pain—should I call about this or shouldn't I? If I didn't, was I putting my life on the line again? Was it normal? Was it abnormal? Saturday night, the cramping grew worse. Two Darvocet didn't touch it. At 11:00, I got out of bed and blood and clots poured out of me. I could literally feel cramps pushing pieces of something out of my body, much like giving birth. I was frightened. No one had told me that this could happen. Once again, a terror of "was I going to die?" consumed me. And once again, all I could think was, *"it's almost midnight; you are NOT going to bother Dr. Carol with this, by having her beeped."* I called for Chuck at that point, and he came in and helped me get up from the toilet. I promptly passed out, came to, and he took me to bed. Then, for the next two hours, we took trips to the bathroom, to monitor what was happening. Eventually it stopped. I found out later, a placenta will grow in the uterus even though the baby grows in the tube and as hormone levels drop, the placenta has to be passed, in something very similar to a miscarriage.

With a ruptured ectopic pregnancy there is more than losing a baby. There is a trauma that comes with knowing you almost waited too long and almost died as a result. It digs deep into your psyche. It's a black cloud that envelops you in a rip-tide of grief, which keeps trying to pull you out to sea. It makes even normal things, ever after, carry a threat of something much more serious, if left too long. You begin to question everything, "Is this normal or is it serious? Will it pass or is this something that, if I ignore it, will threaten my life?" It brings about a fear that at any given moment, your life can be radically and horribly changed - blindsided by grief.

The following are excerpts from my journal in the 12 weeks that followed:

"I am alone on an ocean with no navigational charts that show me how to plot my way through the journey. Even the internet yields very little as far as what to expect emotionally and physically. In the midst of the grief and the ocean rip-tide pulling me under, I find a heart cry, 'Don't let this grief be wasted! God, use this somehow! Give it purpose!' I'm not ready for my grief and experience to be used yet—I'm still trying not to drown myself—but in the future, I want God to use this. How? I don't know. All I know is even now, in this place of pain, I am making myself available to Him by lifting up my fear, my aftermath trauma, my grief, and my empty womb and arms and saying, 'Do with it what you will. Direct me to the people that have a use for my story so that others can find hope. Show me how this is to be used. I'm available. I will wait for you to show me.' Meanwhile, as I wait, I weep and I pace and write and write and write. I hold my daughter close and I tell my husband what I haven't all these months—that I let him down by resenting him and not praying for him. I surrender and trust even as I grieve and mourn. I don't feel like I will make it beyond this, but I know, by His grace, I will. Abandoned surrender. . ."

On another day:

"Chuck has no feeling either way on the baby's sex, but I dreamt of a boy named 'Nathaniel' last night. And so, my heart has forever named our baby 'Nathaniel.' I looked it up. It means 'Gift of God'. I'm not sure yet how this horrific experience is our gift, but I trust I will with time. Abandoned surrender..."

One day, after going to do the dishes, I fell on my knees because the grief came in a rip-tide and carried me away again. I later wrote in my journal:

"Pregnancy is such a happy event. That positive pregnancy test. . . The ecstatic feeling of having a dream come true. . . Writing that first letter to your baby as soon as you become aware of their existence, to put in the baby book. . . Waking up the next morning and remembering you got a miracle growing in you. . . Making the announcement. . .The congratulations. . .Talking with your spouse and daydreaming about your future child. . . Instead of a positive pregnancy test done in the privacy of my own home, I got the news in a phone call in a hospital ultrasound room. Instead of the joyous voice of my Doctor telling me the news, her voice held a somber, serious tone as she told me. I have no ultrasound picture, other than one of a belly full of blood. No pregnancy due date from the Doctor with a big congratulations on it - just hospital papers that tell me how to care for the incision. The only belly I had came from a lopsided bloating as the baby grew on one side, the huge bloating the day I was full of blood, and the post-op bloating. The only cards I have is a huge pile of sympathy cards - - sitting next to bouquets of dying flowers that only emphasize my grief. I think, 'I should throw those away so I don't have to see them.' In the next breath I think, 'I'm going to save those in a keepsake box, so I have something to remember the baby by.'

I didn't get to write that first, euphoric letter. I didn't get to talk to our little one as he lay nestled in my womb. The only conversation I had with him was while I was lying in the "holding room" before surgery, all alone, knowing he was there, but he was already gone. When his warm, safe cocoon burst open, his life ended. Instead of joy and expectation, it was a pregnancy that had only excruciating pain and horrible fear and shock surrounding it. I didn't get one minute of happiness. Not one. The one thing that should so very happy, was only full of sadness, pain, and down-right trauma.

Today, I just can't stop crying. I went to do the dishes and the next thing I knew, I was on the floor next to the sink crying, because my physical heart literally hurt, the grief was so intense. I laid Miracle down for her nap, and I went to the couch and cried some more. I was too incapacitated to do anything but sit and cry. My husband came home briefly, and I cried in his arms. I choked out, 'I wanted that baby so very bad. . . and I didn't even know he was with me! I didn't even know so I could love him for the brief time I had him!'"

And that, is what I can't get past in this grieving process. . .I didn't even have time to love him. And finally, when my healing did began to take place, more questions came: "Why would a woman, who has been told that her chances for pregnancy are slim without medical intervention, get pregnant on her own, only to lose the baby in a ruptured ectopic pregnancy?" This question I have repeatedly brought before the Lord, in the days following our loss, when the grief in my heart becomes too much to bear. "Wasn't infertility enough of a cross to bear? Why would we get a miracle pregnancy only to have it result in such a physically and emotionally painful life-threatening, trauma-filled event, only to end with post-operative pain and the glaring emptiness of my womb and arms?" "God, why? Why would you do this? Why let us even get pregnant?" This is hardly the first time I've asked these questions.

As a woman, who belongs to a blog-ring of other women also experiencing infertility, I have seen the euphoria of positive pregnancy tests, and then the devastation of loss a few weeks and months later. Each time, I have wept with my friends who have experienced such grief. I have felt that same grief shoot into the core of my soul, where it has become my own. As I have tasted the bitterness, I have often thrown questions before God.

Five days before we lost our little one, one of my friends lost her son at 31 weeks pregnancy. Why? Why does God let a woman be pregnant for 31 weeks . . . a woman who's had difficult pregnancies and losses to begin with, and then take that baby? Why? Why does God let a woman, who has tried to get pregnant for seven years, get pregnant, only to take that baby 8 weeks later? Why? Why does God let another woman go through miscarriage after miscarriage? How much loss can one Mama's heart take?

Sitting here, as I write, these words are spoken to my heart: "Your child is with me, the perfect Daddy. You can't hold him, but I can. The love you feel is nothing compared to the love your little one is receiving from me in this very moment. Your children belong to me. Your daughter, who I'm letting you have on earth, and those I chose to take home with me. Life exists on more than 'earth Melissa.' There is life in a realm you cannot see and cannot grasp. I have as much purpose for your children in heaven as I do for your child on earth. Your daughter's life is for earthly purposes — this baby's is for heavenly purposes. This child's life was destined for life in heaven instead of life on earth. This is not only true of your child, but of every child that has been lost. What looks like a senseless act of creating and then destroying, is not so. It is simply creating so that I may then use that child in the destiny I have for them — earthly or heavenly. I reveal this to you, so that you can give others who feel it makes no sense, the same hope. These are lives ordained for heaven and you are the earthly parents ordained for heaven's children."

Melissa Carswell
Owego, New York

When I was 20 years old, I was care free. I thought "nothing can happen. I'm invincible," like almost every other 20 year old thinks. I had been with my boyfriend, since I was 17 years old. His name is Raymond, and he is still the love of my life. Before I became sexually active, I was told by a gynecologist that I had endometriosis, and would have an incredibly hard time getting pregnant. The doctor didn't know if I would even be able to at all. Even at that young age, it made me incredibly sad to hear this, because I did have a dream of having my own family someday. This is where my journey with God began.

One day, I started feeling extremely nauseous, so I went to the store and bought some Pepto Bismol, but for the first time, I noticed it wasn't helping. A couple of days passed, and I was still very sick. I couldn't keep anything down, and I mean ANYTHING! My boyfriend suggested that I should take a pregnancy test just for giggles. We went to Wal-mart, bought the test, and I went into the bathroom right there to use it. It came out POSITIVE! I took another 5 tests, before we finally admitted that I must be pregnant. I cried all the way home, because I didn't know what to do. I knew that I wanted to keep my baby from that very moment, but I was so afraid of how my parents would react. When my mom came home, she saw me crying, and asked me what was wrong. I said simply, "Mom, I'm pregnant." I was only 20 years old and still living at home, so it was a very big shock for my parents. Let's just say that they weren't too happy.

Every night, I prayed to God that my little boy would be okay. I prayed that God would guide me in every decision I made, and help me to be the best mother I could be. Abortion was not an option for me. I knew that life would never be the same again, but on the other hand, I also knew that I would have much joy and happiness. The weeks went by, and finally, everyone was getting more and more excited. Both sets of parents came to accept it. Ray couldn't wait to be a daddy, and I couldn't wait to hold and cuddle my baby. I was having a hard time understanding all of the changes that were happening to my body. My "friends" would often make fun of me, because I couldn't go out and party, and because, well.., I was getting a baby belly. It was hard, and I would cry a lot, because I didn't understand how people could be so cruel. I asked God to hold my hand through all of this.

Physically, everything was going okay up to this point. I had some spotting and cramping, but nothing that was concerning, until I was 25 weeks along. I went to the bathroom, and all it took was one push, and the membranes came out. My, now, fiancé was home with me, when this happened. I was scared to death and in a panic, so, my fiancé called 911. The EMS rushed me to the hospital, where I was told that I would have to be induced for labor, because I still wasn't dilated enough to push the baby out. The doctor broke my water, and gave me medication to force my body into labor. I was in terrible pain, but I didn't want a sedative, because I was afraid that I would be asleep, when my little boy was born. I didn't want to miss seeing him. It was top priority for me.

At this point, I couldn't understand why God was punishing me, in such a terrible way. After I had stopped crying and screaming, the doctor gave me a sedative, and I fell asleep. After 6 hours of labor, I had my little boy. He was still-born. My fiancé and I were able to take pictures of him, hold him, talk to him, and stare at him. I didn't want to let go, and I thought he was precious, just the way he was. It was the hardest day of my life. I thought I had done everything right. I questioned God for awhile.

Four days later, we had a memorial service and burial for him. I was so thankful that God had given me the strength to go through all of that, and thankful that our families were so supportive during this time. My son was born, and joined the angels on July 11, 2009.

In 2010, much to my surprise, I got pregnant again, this time, with a little girl. We named her Sophia Ray (after her daddy, as his name is Raymond Christopher). I had gotten the Trans-abdominal Cerclage (TAC) placed this time at 13 weeks, and everything was going fantastic. This time around, I was gaining weight, not throwing up as much, and I had no spotting at all. We were sure we'd bring our little girl home, instead of a just a memory box. However, when we went for our 20 week ultrasound to find out her gender, we got the most shocking news that parents could get. Our little girl no longer had a heartbeat.

Two weeks before that, I had developed a rash. When I went to my OB, he dismissed it. A week later, I went back again. I was concerned that the rash hadn't gone away. The doctor was mad that I was bothering him with it again, and treated me badly. I asked for an ultrasound, and he refused. He didn't even check for a fetal heartbeat. So when I went to this ultrasound, expecting to find out my baby's gender, and we got the other news instead, I was so in such a state of shock that I couldn't cry.

I have a blood disorder called Von Willebrand Disease, which is like hemophilia. My hospital here did not want to deal with me, because of the disease and because of the Trans Abdominal Cerclage. They said that the doctor didn't feel comfortable, so after they had me waiting in the hospital from 12 PM until 1 AM in the morning, I was sent to a hospital one hour away. When I got there, they worked on me like a lab rat. They had about 10 doctors look at me, and they did about 4 ultrasounds "just to make sure." I went through the agony of seeing the precious little girl that I wasn't going to take home another five times. They decided they would not do a c-section, and that instead, they would remove my TAC. I was devastated! I wouldn't even get to see my little girl because they would have to do a D& C. I completely broke down at the hospital - I didn't eat, didn't talk to anyone, and was angry and mean.

We lost Sophia Ray on November 3, 2010. Once I left the hospital, I again questioned God many times. I wondered what I did that was so horrible to be worthy of me losing my two babies. I wondered why He would do something so terrible to me and my fiancé. I asked "why" a thousand times, and I became jealous of everyone else that had a normal and healthy pregnancy.

Two weeks after I left the hospital, I had fallen into such a deep depression that I tried to commit suicide. I was back in the hospital for seven days. At the hospital, I knew that God was protecting me, and I felt at peace - even if it was for just a short time. Once I got out, many things changed. It wasn't right away, but a few months down the road, I started to realize that God didn't punish me. I started to believe that everything happens for a reason. I asked God to help me find comfort, and happiness in my life. I asked Him to help me to not forget my children, but to learn to live with what had happened - learn to accept it and to mourn in a healthy way.

I have learned so many things. One of them is that a lot of people do not care about my loss, or they do not think it was a loss and act as if I should get over it. God has helped me so much with this. I know that if He wasn't watching over me, I would still be very depressed, especially from hearing all of these things - sometimes even from family members (not my parents or immediate family, but aunts etc.). I can now talk openly about God, and help other women. I think that He had a mission planned for me to complete in this world. It included allowing me to go through terrible heartbreak, so that I can help other women, who have experienced the same things. It may sound bad, but talking to others in this same situation has helped me to heal. It makes me happy to think that I can help others, because I have gone through such pain.

I will never forget my children. I will always love them, and keep them in my heart and memories. I know that they will be waiting at heaven's gates with my Lord and Savior, and one day, I will FINALLY get to be their mother.

Dominique Naudy
Monroe, New York

Chapter 6

The Miracle of Sharing

In this life, some situations are easy to share with others, and some are not. As I mentioned earlier, I *needed* to share this loss with those around me. I needed the support and the prayers of my family and friends. Often, when we are in the midst of trials, we find it difficult to express to God what is deep within our hearts. I found comfort in the thought that God provided a way through intercessory prayer and through His Holy Spirit.

Romans 8:26-27 - Likewise the Spirit also helpeth our infirmities: for we know not what we should pray for as we ought: but the Spirit itself maketh intercession for us with groanings which cannot be uttered. And he that searcheth the hearts knoweth what is the mind of the Spirit, because he maketh intercession for the saints according to the will of God.

One of the most difficult aspects of this whole process was carrying my dead child in my womb through the weekend, until my surgery. Until I was scheduled for a D&C, I had never even heard of the procedure before. I spent many hours researching miscarriages and the information surrounding them. Also, I had only met one or two women, who I knew had had a miscarriage, and it was never a topic of major discussion. I was terrified! I quickly discovered that even though I could not find very much organized information on the subject, the more I was willing to share with those around me, the more others would share with me. As heartbreaking as it was (and still is) to hear the stories of others' losses, it ministered to me in a way that nothing else could. Just knowing that others had felt this pain, had worked through it, and had come out on the other side gave me hope. I found that as I shared my story, it was accompanied by less tears and more smiles each time. God definitely used the prior struggles of friends and acquaintances around me, to bring peace to my heart and comfort to my soul.

I quickly found the courage to listen to and obey God, as He was prompting me to speak at my MOPS group. I wanted to thank the wonderful women, who God had placed at my table, for their love, help, and support. I hardly knew these beautiful Moms, but they were Jesus to me and my family in the weeks following the passing of baby Brooks. I did not write a speech or prepare anything fancy to say at that meeting, but I let God give me the words to share what I was learning, even just a short time after my loss. After my brief testimony, I was touched by the women who thanked me for sharing. Later, I was told that one woman, extremely depressed over a recent miscarriage, was completely blessed and encouraged in a way she had not been, since her loss. What an opportunity to bless another hurting woman through my own loss! It amazed me how God could take something so seemingly devastating, and fashion something so incredibly positive out of it.

Another wonderful opportunity that was given to me through this situation was that of sharing with my unsaved family and friends. Because people knew of my pain, they were exceptionally willing to listen and to give me 100% of their attention. Many of these people would not have listened to talk about God under ordinary circumstances. No one wants to be rude to someone who is going through a traumatic experience. I have been given the chance to share over and over again of God's unending love, grace, and peace in the midst of my pain and grief. Actually, it was during this time that God spoke to my heart about writing a book. I never would have developed the vision to write a book like this on my own. I had written poems and some teen material for Sunday school, but besides that, nothing much larger than a standard term paper for college. I wasn't so sure that I was ready for the size of this commitment, but I decided to at least work out a basic outline. It completely blew my mind how quickly the words came. Not only did I have the outline, I also had the bones of this book written in a matter of a few weeks. This was truly God's plan for me. My heart ached for the numerous women that I was meeting – almost daily, it seemed – who were hurting and empty, after the loss of a child or children. I felt that if God could use my pain to bring peace and hope to another, it would make these difficult days matter for eternity.

How often do we hear people ask, "Why does a good God allow evil to happen – especially to 'good' people?" This question is at the root of what we believe as born-again Christians. Once again, Lordship is the answer. We must have the faith to believe that what God allows and what he brings into our lives is *always* for our good – a small piece of a large puzzle.

> *Romans 8:28* - *And we know that all things work together for good to them that love God, to them who are the called according to his purpose.*

He also uses those things in our lives to grow us and teach us, just as a parent does for a child. He *allowed* sin to enter into the world, with the full knowledge of it. It was not His perfect way, but He did not choose to create "robots" either. He finds pleasure and delight in us, when we *choose* to do what honors Him. Most of all, when we are within the boundaries of His will, *everything* that happens in our life is designed to bring the most possible glory to Himself. It is not about me or you – it is *all* about Him.

> ***Psalm 30:11-12*** *- Thou hast turned for me my mourning into dancing: thou hast put off my sackcloth, and girded me with gladness; To the end that my glory may sing praise to thee, and not be silent. O LORD my God, I will give thanks unto thee for ever.*

> ***1 Corinthians 10:31*** *- Whether therefore ye eat, or drink, or whatsoever ye do, do all to the glory of God.*

> ***Luke 19:37-40*** *- And when he was come nigh, even now at the descent of the mount of Olives, the whole multitude of the disciples began to rejoice and praise God with a loud voice for all the mighty works that they had seen; Saying, Blessed be the King that cometh in the name of the Lord: peace in heaven, and glory in the highest. And some of the Pharisees from among the multitude said unto him, Master, rebuke thy disciples. And he answered and said unto them, I tell you that, if these should hold their peace, the stones would immediately cry out.*

Another wonderful result of sharing my story is how I believe that it will continue to minister to my immediate family in the future. Long ago, I promised myself that my children would hear "I love you" a million times more than they could ever want to. I also decided that I would try to avoid following those special words with a "but..." (For example: "I love you, but you need to be good.") I find this can be difficult at times; however, somehow that transitional "but" tends to invalidate the adoring words of love.

I believe that truly loving your children *unconditionally* – with actions and also with words – cannot be replaced with anything else. I know how much those little words mean to me, even as an adult. It seems that sharing with my earthly children about my experience and the love that I have for my heavenly children will only further show them how much they mean to me. Caring about and desiring my children, from the moment they were conceived, also teaches them the importance of the sanctity of life, and the importance of fighting for it, in this world of disillusioned people, who would rather save a whale, a tree, or even a body of water than the life of an unborn human-being.

If our children come to embrace a strong respect for human life, hopefully, we will have an easier time explaining abstinence before marriage, the pain of abortion, and the importance of reaching their peers for Christ. As parents, I feel that we need to use every opportunity– both the good and the difficult, which God sends to us or allows in our lives, to teach and to train our children.

> ***Deuteronomy 6:1a,7*** *- Now these are the command-ments, the statutes, and the judgments, which the LORD your God commanded to teach you, ... And thou shalt teach them diligently unto thy children, and shalt talk of them when thou sittest in thine house, and when thou walkest by the way, and when thou liest down, and when thou risest up.*

Ultimately, our faith in God and our belief that He has our best interest at heart, should allow us to share our experi-ences and our heartaches with true abandon and total peace, desiring always to bring glory and honor to our Lord and Savior, Jesus Christ. Our God is not the author of confu-sion, and what He allows to happen is within His ability to control and even manipulate, if He so chooses. Knowing this fact should strengthen our testimony before those around us, who are searching for peace and direction amidst the calamities of life.

1 Corinthians 14:33a - For God is not the author of confusion, but of peace...

Proverbs 21: 1 - The king's heart is in the hand of the LORD, as the rivers of water: he turneth it whithersoever he will.

Ephesians 1:11- In whom also we have obtained an inheritance, being predestinated according to the purpose of him who worketh all things after the counsel of his own will.

M y story happened well over 40 years ago in between my first and second child. The miscarriage I had occurred around 8 weeks into my pregnancy. As I recall, it was not very eventful, but just happened at home in the bathroom. I called the doctor, and a forthcoming D&C was performed.

I definitely felt the loss of another child that I wanted, but my Christian experience and my nursing experience at that time, told me that this was the Lord's will, and that circumstances must not have been right to carry this child to term. I surrendered this experience to the Lord's will and moved on with my life.

It was much later in my life and Christian growth that I fully realized that one day when I got to heaven and met my Lord and Savior that that miscarried, unborn child would *be there - whole* and *complete*. Then, I would meet him or her for the very first time. I am so looking forward to meeting my fourth child at that time. The reality of this is truly a joyful *hope* and *expectation,* which I have as a follower of Jesus Christ and in the promise of His Word.

Linda Besser
Venice, Florida

M y sister told me this, "God is merciful. He shows mercy to a baby that may have been unhealthy, and mercy to parents who would have had to bear the pain of a sick child. Just think of the mercy God has shown you and the baby." (She has 2 perfect daughters, as well as 3 babies in heaven.)

I lost one baby, and still think of him/her sometimes. It is still painful even after having 2 other children. I will never understand why things happened the way they did, but I know I will meet my baby someday, all grown up and perfect in heaven.

Life is precious, and life is a gift.

Emily Nelson
Apalachin, New York

My first miscarriage was a total shock because I had 0 symptoms (no cramping, bleeding, etc...) I thought everything was fine and went in for my 10 week ultrasound (first visit to the doctor). My mom came with me because Nathan my husband was teaching a class, and we didn't suspect a thing. I had the ultrasound and the doctor got really quiet for a long time. She quietly told me there was no heartbeat. It didn't really sink in what had happened, and we talked briefly about what we should do. I didn't want to make any decisions on the spot so we just talked about options and set up another appointment for the next week. The doctor left and my mom came in. I was changing behind the curtain and my mom asked excitedly how it looked. I could barely get any words out I was so stunned, but I remember just saying bitterly "Mom, the baby is dead." We went back to school, and I waited for Nathan to get out of his class to tell him. He was stunned too and we went home for the rest of the day to try to comprehend what had happened. All that next week we hoped my body would miscarry naturally, but I had no show of anything at all.

The first week was surreal with the encouragement of people and reassurance of prayers, but a small ache started to form and questions started to gather in the back of my mind. At my next doctor's visit the doctor measured the baby and said it really appeared to have died at 8 weeks, so I had been carrying it around for 3 full weeks with no sign of miscarriage. She felt that I needed a D&C to take care of it. I was very afraid to have surgery like that, but we could clearly see that the baby was lifeless, and so I had the surgery. I was relieved going into it that they would take the baby because walking around knowing you were carrying a dead baby was hard to deal with. But as soon as I came out of the surgery I started sobbing and asked for the baby back. I was starting to realize that it was a life and a part of Nathan and I, and I missed it even after just a few weeks of carrying it.

People gave us lots of verses and words of comfort, but the thing that got me through that first experience was something Nathan pointed out to me one afternoon at Lake Robinson. Nathan and I have made it our goal as a couple to point as many people to Christ as possible with our lives. He said that there was significant scriptural evidence that babies are taken to heaven, and he was encouraged because he considered our miscarriage a contribution to the population in heaven. It is a wonderful thing to be able to help populate heaven by witnessing and leading a soul to Christ, but it became a realization to us that we had also helped to bring a soul to Christ by conceiving and allowing God to take the child. We decided to name the baby "Treasure" — our treasure in heaven.

Matthew 6:20-21 - "Lay up for yourselves treasures in heaven where neither moth nor rust destroys and where thieves do not break in and steal. For where your treasure is, there your heart will be also."

That was a sweet time for us, but then things turned dark as we got a month out from the miscarriage. The weekend the baby died, I had confronted a friend about some pretty major problems in her life that had been building for over a year. Her parents had begged me to talk to her many times, and I finally relented. Her response took me by surprise and hurt me more deeply than anything I could remember before. I expected her to either recognize the problem and be willing to get help, or to get angry and refuse to listen. Instead, she piously accused me of being "unbiblical" and assured me that she was confident that her life and actions were in the will of God. Her spiritual sounding accusations and false assurance of God's will were so appalling and hurtful to me that I really fell apart emotionally that weekend as I realized how committed she was to her sin.

Although I didn't find out until two weeks later, the baby had died that weekend. As I put the time line together in my mind, I started to be overcome with guilt and anger. I started wondering if I had killed the baby by allowing my emotions to overcome me. I was angry that my effort to help a friend had cost a life. I loved my friend, but she was not worth any life much less the life of my child. A Christian nurse assured me I had not "killed" the baby. She comforted me that babies are very strong and resilient, and that even if my emotional weekend had stressed the baby and been the catalyst to its death, that it would have died at some point anyway, because there was some other problem - either genetically or hormonally. That was something I could not control. I have overcome the guilt of the miscarriage, but I don't know that I can honestly say I have overcome the bitterness towards my friend. I go through times when I feel I can completely forgive her for her response, but then there are moments when I still have a hint of anger rise up in my heart and it takes some amount of effort to give that back to the Lord.

Almost a year later I was pregnant again. This time I had an ultrasound at 6 weeks because of my previous miscarriage. Everything looked good. Then, I started bleeding. Not a lot and not very consistent, but still it was there. I called my mom, and I was so afraid it was happening again. The doctor's office said to just go home and rest. My mom reminded me that the baby's life was in God's hands, and there was nothing I could or couldn't do to prevent another miscarriage. I just had to relax in His will – I had no other options.

At 7 weeks, I had another ultrasound and everything looked good. We could see a heartbeat! The doctor said a lot of people have spotting during pregnancy. The next entire week, I read blog after blog looking for a pattern in people's experience as to whether or not bleeding meant an imminent miscarriage. The outcome was totally inconclusive. Some people had lots of bleeding and delivered a healthy baby and some people had spotting and miscarried the next day. As the week progressed the bleeding seemed to lighten so my hopes grew. At 8 weeks, I had my third ultrasound. My heart stopped as the doctor said there was no heartbeat. It HAD happened again. I was able to partially miscarry that week, and then, the doctor was able to clear out the little that remained at her office. This time, it was not such a shock but more a feeling of defeat. For me, it was easier the second time. I knew more what to expect physically and emotionally. I never lost hope that we would have children, but Nathan did. He started to think through what we would do with our lives if we didn't have kids. He started to mention adoption. Again people offered comfort and encouragement. This time though, I felt more relaxed and peaceful, because I knew that my child's life was completely in the Lord's hands, and we had once again contributed a soul to heaven. The verse that encouraged me the most this time was:

John 14:27 - *"Peace I leave with you; my peace I give you. Not as the world gives do I give you. Let not your hearts be troubled, neither let them be afraid."*

The Lord had taken another child, but he left peace in my heart, and we didn't need to fear the future. We named the second baby "Peace." It takes time to heal, but healing does come with time. I was able to talk freely of the miscarriages and move on, although we always try to remember their short lives. When people ask us if we have children, we try to say, "yes, two in heaven".

I got pregnant a third time, and my doctor had me take progesterone during my first trimester. Whether or not that was the problem the first two times, we don't know, but we now have a healthy baby boy named "Shepherd" from Psalm 23. We have no idea how much time the Lord will give us with this child, but we know that whatever happens, He will take care of us just as he did with the first two pregnancies.

Abigail Crocket
Taylors, South Carolina

⤙ Chapter 7 ⤚

The Miracle of Truth

B y early January 2010, we were pregnant again. Once
again, the sickness picked up with a fury. I never
thought I would dislike being pregnant. I had had such an
enjoyable time during my first pregnancy, but now, after
months of being stuck in a vicious cycle of sickness and
exhaustion, pain and frustration, and celebration and disappointment, I was ready to call it quits! It certainly was not
that I did not *want* to be pregnant, or that I did not *want* a
baby – unquestionably, I wanted both! I was just so miserable that I struggled to reflect on the positive attributes of
my current situation. After many long months of being nauseous 24/7, I finally "gave in," and asked my doctor for some
anti-nausea medication. I still felt sick most of each day, but
at least I could eat a meal and avoid any extra trips to the
bathroom. (Bathroom breaks already seem to consume over
half of a pregnant woman's day!) I decided that not only
would I need to learn how to *survive* this new way of life
called "pregnancy," but I would also need to learn how to
enjoy it, in spite of the additional complications that would
be involved this time around.

My health was definitely not my only new challenge. I
soon found that having a toddler running around – at top
speed with no "off switch" – was a lot harder than I could
have imagined. My hat goes off to pregnant women who

already have three, four, or even more little ones! I have always struggled with feelings of inadequacy, but I was swimming in them now. I couldn't even keep up with the energy level of my little guy, not to mention trying to teach him things such as letters, numbers, shapes, or potty training. (By the way, I do not understand why the children get the candy or the stickers for going on the potty. Why don't the moms get anything – like a trophy or an honorary degree or something?) Knowing that my son was still young and would never remember my multitude of "short-comings" during this time did help comfort me a little bit. The time I had *alone* with Channing was drawing to a close. I wanted to enjoy each and every moment – because unlike my forgetful little boy, *I would remember*.

Another difficulty that I faced, during this time, was my distorted views and attitudes. I still continue to struggle with these issues at times, as I always have, but the hormones and fatigue greatly contributed to the daily battle I had to wage against the lies that attacked my mind, and the way I reacted to them. The first area, in particular, that I struggled with was my short-comings as a wife. I am married to my best friend and the most wonderful man I could have wished for. I often felt so undeserving of his love for me. I wish that I had his unending patience and forgiveness, which he quietly bestows upon me, each and every day. I found myself continually dwelling on my "failures" – a dish left in the sink, dog prints on the hardwood floors, dust in the corners, or clutter in the closet. Once again, I was finding my significance in things around me, instead of in the One that created me.

I have always had a problem with controlling my temper, which usually crescendos into unkind outbursts directed towards those I love. During pregnancy, my fuse was especially short. Daily, I would find myself losing my temper over simple things that didn't go my way or tasks that were not completed to my high standard of satisfaction. I said things to my son and to my husband that I didn't mean. Undoubtedly, they did not deserve my attitude towards them. During this time of my life, with its hormones, mood swings, medication changes, and emotional distress, many more regrettable moments have been added to my life. I sometimes found myself wondering if another child was really what I needed right then. Obviously, it was much too late to think about that, but the thought still plagued me. Was I going to be like this forever? Could I learn patience fast enough to handle another child? Would I end up breaking my children's spirits with my impatient frustrations? Would I destroy my marriage or alienate my husband with my words or my attitude? "God, please help me!" became the cry of my heart. It was the only thing that I could manage to say. I share my feelings candidly and without reserve, in the hope that someone may find comfort in the fact that they are not alone.

1 Corinthians 10:13 - There hath no temptation taken you but such as is common to man: but God is faithful, who will not suffer you to be tempted above that ye are able; but will with the temptation also make a way to escape, that ye may be able to bear it.

I knew that God was able to change my heart and my attitudes, if I would let Him. I was ready. Change came. Slow at first, but soon, I was surprised that others were commenting on my attitude and how different I was. Since then, God has done an amazing work in my life and has significantly changed my attitudes and expectations, and I find myself looking on the "bright side" much more often now. I even find that I can control my temper much better, and, often, I even think before I speak, though I wouldn't say that I always heed my own cautions. This area will always be a difficult one for me, and though my past circumstances are often the reason I act or react in a particular way, I have come to learn that it is *never* an excuse for bad behavior.

Though I still consider this area to be the source of many of my past and present regrets, I did feel the greater part of my negativity and critical thinking slowly melting away. Not only did God remove the bad attitude associated with my recent losses, but He also took away the negativity and bitterness that I held from my past. Even now, however, it is so easy to try to take back control, and allow my arrogance to keep me from becoming the mother and the wife that I long to be. I also find that I allow my failures, fears, and disappointments to diminish and, often, even eradicate the blessings that God intended to give to me. I need to remember to be affirmative towards myself and others, and to concentrate on the truth about each situation that I face. I need to stop wasting time distressing about my past and my future, and just begin to take life one day at a time. Again, there needs to be a fine balance of preparing for what *could* happen and looking forward, with hope, to what *will* happen. Often, it's all about perspective.

Matthew 6: 25-34 - Therefore I say unto you, Take no thought for your life, what ye shall eat, or what ye shall drink; nor yet for your body, what ye shall put on. Is not the life more than meat, and the body than raiment? Behold the fowls of the air: for they sow not, neither do they reap, nor gather into barns; yet your heavenly Father feedeth them. Are ye not much better than they? Which of you by taking thought can add one cubit unto his stature? And why take ye thought for raiment? Consider the lilies of the field, how they grow; they toil not, neither do they spin: And yet I say unto you, That even Solomon in all his glory was not arrayed like one of these. Wherefore, if God so clothe the grass of the field, which to day is, and to morrow is cast into the oven, shall he not much more clothe you, O ye of little faith? Therefore take no thought, saying, What shall we eat? or, What shall we drink? or, Wherewithal shall we be clothed? (For after all these things do the Gentiles seek:) for your heavenly Father knoweth that ye have need of all these things. But seek ye first the kingdom of God, and his righteousness; and all these things shall be added unto you. Take therefore no thought for the morrow: for the morrow shall take thought for the things of itself. Sufficient unto the day is the evil thereof.

As I pause to consider my blessings, four amazing things concerning my loss come to mind almost immediately. First of all, I have the wonderful reassurance that my sweet babies will never know the pain and heartache – physical or emotional – that I have experienced throughout my life. They will never know evil, temptation, or guilt.

Ecclesiastes 4:1-3 - So I returned, and considered all the oppressions that are done under the sun: and behold the tears of such as were oppressed, and they had no comforter; and on the side of their oppressors there was power; but they had no comforter. Wherefore I praised the dead which are already dead more than the living which are yet alive. Yea, better is he than both they, which hath not yet been, who hath not seen the evil work that is done under the sun.

Second, my babies opened their beautiful little eyes for the first time to see the face of Jesus. What more could a Mother desire for her children? They passed into eternity without ever touching this broken and difficult world – to a completely perfect life. The following passage describes this transformation:

1 Corinthians 15:50-55 - *Now this I say, brethren, that flesh and blood cannot inherit the kingdom of God; neither doth corruption inherit incorruption. Behold, I shew you a mystery; We shall not all sleep, but we shall all be changed, In a moment, in the twinkling of an eye, at the last trump: for the trumpet shall sound, and the dead shall be raised incorruptible, and we shall be changed. For this corruptible must put on incorruption, and this mortal must put on immortality. So when this corruptible shall have put on incorruption, and this mortal shall have put on immortality, then shall be brought to pass the saying that is written, Death is swallowed up in victory. O death, where is thy sting? O grave, where is thy victory?*

Third, what a relief it is to know that I will never need to fear for their health, their safety, or especially their spiritual condition. God took care of every single aspect of their well-being in an instant. It may not have been the way that I would have chosen, or the plan I would have devised, but He did not allow me that choice. He fulfilled *His* plan *His* way.

1 Corinthians 1:26-28 - For ye see your calling, brethren, how that not many wise men after the flesh, not many mighty, not many noble, are called: But God hath chosen the foolish things of the world to confound the wise; and God hath chosen the weak things of the world to confound the things which are mighty; And base things of the world, and things which are despised, hath God chosen, yea, and things which are not, to bring to nought things that are:

The fourth and final wonderful thing that I have come to understand is how blessed I am to have been chosen for this "task." Often, we hear people say that "we do not know why

God allowed 'this' or 'that' to happen." However, I would like to suggest that *everything* happens for the purpose of bringing glory to God. Consider the story of Lazarus:

> **John 11:1-4** - *Now a certain man was sick, named Lazarus, of Bethany, the town of Mary and her sister Martha. (It was that Mary which anointed the Lord with ointment, and wiped his feet with her hair, whose brother Lazarus was sick.) Therefore his sisters sent unto him, saying, Lord, behold, he whom thou lovest is sick. When Jesus heard that, he said, This sickness is not unto death, but for the glory of God, that the Son of God might be glorified thereby.*

The passage goes on to say that Lazarus did indeed die, causing many people to question the ability and the compassion of Jesus. However, in the end, Jesus used this opportunity to show the extent of His power, by bringing Lazarus back to life. Though He may have many other reasons for allowing things to happen as they do, I truly believe that the *ultimate* reason for all things is to bring glory to God and to show us His omnipotence.

God knew before the time of conception that these children would never know earthly parents. He wanted to bring glory to Himself through the short and *seemingly* insignificant lives of these little ones. We know that the scriptures teach that Jesus loves children, and I have no doubt that He finds great joy in their company. Who is to say that He may not create some children just for Himself?

> **Matthew 19:13-15** - *Then were there brought unto him little children, that he should put his hands on them, and pray: and the disciples rebuked them. But Jesus said, Suffer little children, and forbid them not, to come unto me: for of such is the kingdom of heaven.*

Matthew 21:16 *- And said unto him, Hearest thou what these say? And Jesus saith unto them, Yea; have ye never read, Out of the mouth of babes and sucklings thou hast perfected praise?*

I praise God that I was given an opportunity such as this. I have seen so many other wonderful things come from this difficult time in my life, but ultimately, I have been amazed at the glory God has received. I have no doubt that it has been *His* hand guiding me through it all.

As a woman, who always longed to be a mother, I found myself honored, during this time, to have had three children with another one on the way. I will always be "Mommy" to all of my children – those I can hold now, as well as those I will meet in heaven, someday in the future.

I found my appreciation for the frailty of life growing, as I worked through my grief. I could truly stand in awe of the little life growing secretly in my womb, and bless God for His plan and purpose for – not only my life – but also for the lives of each of my children.

Psalm 139:13-17 *- For thou hast possessed my reins: thou hast covered me in my mother's womb. I will praise thee; for I am fearfully and wonderfully made: marvellous are thy works; and that my soul knoweth right well. My substance was not hid from thee, when I was made in secret, and curiously wrought in the lowest parts of the earth. Thine eyes did see my substance, yet being unperfect; and in thy book all my members were written, which in continuance were fashioned, when as yet there was none of them. How precious also are thy thoughts unto me, O God! how great is the sum of them!*

I had a miscarriage between Miles & Miller. I saw a healthy heartbeat at my 8 week appointment, and went in for my next routine visit at about 15 weeks along. The heartbeat was gone and had apparently been gone for quite some time. They scheduled me for a D&C the following day. Here's what I wrote on my blog:

"I don't know if anyone actually reads this. I started it more for myself than anyone else, to just jot down memories of the boys, etc. I never thought I'd be posting this very personal memory. Yesterday, at my routine (almost)15 week pre-natal appointment, we found out that our baby no longer had a heartbeat, and had probably been gone for at least several days. The news came as quite a shock, but the Lord was so gracious. My appointment, providentially, was with the doctor who is an elder in our church. He was very compassionate and helped us get the recommended D&C scheduled and completed quickly. Michael's Sunday school teacher is the charge nurse for the O.R., and stayed with me afterwards, until Josh came back. The physical recovery hasn't been bad at all. Physically, I should be back to normal in a couple of days. I had no idea how much this would hurt emotionally, but I'm SO thankful to have Josh & the boys. The boys were a really special joy to us today. The Lord has lifted us up and comforted us through family & friends. We have so much for which to be thankful, and are looking forward to enjoying each other for as many moments as God blesses us."

Heather Pitts
Leesburg, Georgia

G od had given me 2 precious girls, 16 months apart. So, after about 3 ½ years, we were eager to add to our family. I went off birth control, and the next month got pregnant. It would be perfect. We would have a doctor's appointment, and find out right before Christmas, when my parents would be visiting. God had other plans, which were far more perfect.

I had suspected nothing, since I had easily gotten pregnant with the other 2. The doctor did an ultrasound at 10 weeks. She kept searching for a heartbeat. There was none. My little one had gone home at 7 weeks. I didn't know what to think. Praise the Lord for His timing, though. In the van's CD player was Kevin Inafuku's CD, "Love So Amazing." Hearing those songs was exactly what my heart needed. Yes, I cried the whole way home, but I sang and praised God that I was His child, and that I could rest in Him, when my world seemed to be caving in.

Psalm46:10a – *"Be still and know that I am God."*

Kristalyn Lovegrove
Menifee, California

Chapter 8

The Miracle of another Chance

The first trimester of my fourth pregnancy was full of fear and faith – often more fear than faith, unfortunately. I prayed nearly every hour for peace and reassurance as to the outcome of this pregnancy. By now, I was at peace with the past, but it seemed that the only thing my mind could dwell on, now, was the health of this little one inside of me. The day of the first ultrasound at 10 weeks was one of the scariest days of my life. I sat in the waiting room, with my stomach churning and my heart racing. I think my hands were actually melting. Every time the nurse came out to call someone back, I thought I would pass out. Finally, when my turn came, I managed to follow the nurse back to the ultrasound room. As I climbed onto the table, I was still shaking, but as soon as the picture of our little one appeared on the screen, I felt all of my fears vanish. There he was - perfect and beautiful. And then, the wonderful sound of a tiny heartbeat! That's when the tears came. Praise God! He had chosen to allow me to carry *this* tiny child a bit longer.

God certainly cared about my fears and my uncertainties. With my first pregnancy, I didn't feel Channing move until nearly 14 weeks, and then, not regularly until after 20 weeks. This time, I began feeling the tell-tale gurgles around 9 weeks and quite regularly, from then on. This little guy was so active. It was difficult to fear for my baby's life, when he was doing a 24/7 gymnastics routine in my belly. I have heard so many pregnant women whine about their unborn child's boundless energy at 3am, but after my experiences, I was thrilled at every little movement, no matter what time it was. I was certain that this little guy was going to come out sleeping, after all that endless kicking! Channing, very early in this pregnancy, decided to call this baby, "Baby Joy," and we quickly picked up on the nickname. Finally, this pregnancy was becoming a bit more enjoyable, and mentally, I was finally able to relax.

Physically, I continued to deal with the health issues that I had had prior to this pregnancy. My spine had a very difficult time holding up during this pregnancy, and I found myself in severe pain most of the time. I was very limited on what medications I could take. Often, "suffering through with prayer" was the only way to handle it. I also dealt with thyroid issues, which frequently made me very tired, cranky, and just plain miserable. I had had to post-pone increasing my medications, which would have solved these undesirable issues, until after the birth of our child. My doctor actually lowered my dose of thyroid medication, because he felt that my regularly-elevated levels could have caused my previous miscarriages. So, amidst a "screaming" back, weak legs, painful hips, extreme exhaustion, my hair falling out in clumps, and miserable moodiness, I often wondered why God would give me such a heart and a desire for children, but then, make having them so very difficult. Yet, once again, I reminded myself that He has a plan. I have always desired to adopt a child. Maybe this is God's way of eventually forcing that decision. What a blessing it would be to "rescue" a child from a life of sadness, loneliness, and, maybe, even fear and pain. Best of all, what a joy it would be to share my precious Savior with another soul, who may otherwise never hear of Him. My God truly knows how to fulfill His perfect plan in our lives, and I knew He would not fail me now.

During those first few anxious months, I found that there were several difficulties that came with "another chance" to carry a child. First of all, the frustration of the question, "why?" was almost a barrier to enjoying my opportunity to have another child. Often, past experiences determine the response to current and future experiences. Sometimes it is easier to stand on the outside of a situation and make suggestions and judgments about how something should be handled, but when you are on the inside, it is often much more difficult. Before my miscarriages, I had very strong negative opinions about those who had abortions, abandoned their children, cheated on their spouses, had children out of wedlock, or made a multitude of other less-than-perfect choices. God has used the loss of my children to work in my heart. I needed to learn to have compassion on people, and find a way to minister to them exactly where they are. I had to discover ways to put myself into their shoes, and try to understand why they would choose the path that they do. Everyone has a past, and everyone has a story. It was only by the grace of God, that I did not choose one of the same routes.

1 Corinthians 15:10 - But by the grace of God I am what I am: and his grace which was bestowed upon me was not in vain; but I laboured more abundantly than they all: yet not I, but the grace of God which was with me.

As God continued to work on my heart, and my own loss and heartbreak slowly became much more bearable, I found that if I did not waste my time feeling sorry for myself, I had so much more time to concentrate on others. As I spent more time listening to and sharing with others, I discovered that each choice – right or wrong - resulted after a combination of many past experiences – taught, learned, and shared – came together. Often, the first step in healing is not asking "why?" but, rather, it is understanding the "how" behind the "what."

I am still learning to give all of my "why's" to God and trust Him to accomplish His perfect will in my life in spite of my prior "what's." His perfect love can mend a broken and hurting heart – *mine and yours.*

> *Philippians 4:6* - *Be careful for nothing; but in every thing by prayer and supplication with thanksgiving let your requests be made known unto God.*

> *1 John 4:18* - *There is no fear in love; but perfect love casteth out fear: because fear hath torment. He that feareth is not made perfect in love.*

Another obstacle I found to be quite difficult for me to overcome was the question of "How?" How would I tolerate and, then, recover from a fourth pregnancy? I did not realize that having a miscarriage at three months was still very similar, in a number of ways, to giving birth full-term. As I mentioned before, my body had to go through many of the same processes to heal, as I did after the birth of my first child. I also did not realize how much having two abrupt and "repeat-pregnancies" could take out of your body. After the second miscarriage, my body was drained, even though I did not really notice it at the time. When I became pregnant for a third time, just a month and a half after the D&C, I began to feel the effects of this exhaustion catching up with me. It was more like starting at the end of the pregnancy, rather than the beginning. Maybe we should have waited a bit longer to try to conceive, but we truly wanted to leave the timing in God's hands. Obviously, He knew what I could handle, and for some reason, He chose this child at this time. I will say that, after this experience, I completely understand why a typical pregnancy only lasts about 9 months. (Elephants must receive an extra helping of endurance to carry their pregnancies to 22 months!) I was praying and trusting that

God would give me the strength that I knew my body would be lacking to endure the full nine months and then, to heal properly, after the birth of this little one.

The third major struggle, with an additional pregnancy, was the fear of circumstantial "unknowns". I remembered how difficult it was after Channing was born, to feel so very alone while taking care of a child, especially a newborn. I remember the late nights in tears, with no one to talk to. (I do remember yelling at the ceiling a lot, though.) I refused to purposely wake my husband, knowing he needed to go to the office the next day. He could not possibly understand the hormonal roller coaster that I found myself on, not that he didn't try. *I* couldn't even understand it, most of the time. Unfortunately, I still managed to wake him with my wailing, on more than one occasion. He was always so good about taking Channing from me, and sending me to bed. Prayer would have solved a world of problems, and probably solved this issue much sooner, but I was too tired and too frustrated to pray. Anyhow, nine months after the birth of Channing and after falling apart nearly every night, I was finally able to get the help that I so desperately needed for my post-partum depression.

During this time, I did have one particular friend that I must mention. (She was more of an "angel," now that I look back on it.) Nora was almost always there when I was ready to fall through the cracks. We had met through a mutual friend at church. She was a wonderful, sweet, considerate, and thoughtful woman. She was (and still is) one of those extraordinary people that everyone loves, and you could almost literally *see* Jesus pouring out of her. Each time I found myself hanging by a proverbial thread, she would be there – ready to watch Channing anytime and anywhere. She never hesitated to answer God's prodding to call me with an encouraging word, or with an offer to lend a hand. After I called her to tell her about my second miscarriage, she immediately jumped in her car and came to get Channing for the day, allowing me the very necessary opportunity to grieve and to spend time with God, during that first, very challenging, day. My heart is over-whelmed with gratefulness for the way in which God used Nora in my life. Recently, God moved her and her little family to another state, but we keep in touch, and I pray that she will always continue to be a special part of our lives, just as she was during those difficult years.

I absolutely feared being in a circumstance of feeling alone again, and I desperately wanted another *woman's* support this time as well. My family lives in South Carolina, and Kevin's parents spend a good part of each year in Florida. I had only just discovered MOPS, and I only had a couple close friends, at this point - none of whom, I felt comfortable calling on at 3am. I only had the hospital hot-line and God. I guess I underestimated how much "help" that actually was and would be. I was nervous about how I would handle things this time around. I knew I did not want to take any chances with post-partum depression again. I was already taking an anti-depressant, and had every intention of increasing the dose as soon as this little guy popped out, but would that be enough?

Often, I still find myself jealous, as I look around at my friends and acquaintances and at their strong family support systems. I do not know any one of them that struggle for help, or even have to ask for it. They have plenty of date nights with their husbands, and most of them even get frequent over-nights "child-free." They have grandparents, who live nearby, practically knocking down their doors to "borrow" the grandkids. I even hear these parents complain that they do not get to see their own children enough, at times. It is so easy to get caught up in a "pity-party" for myself. Sure, it would be great to have that kind of support system around me, but for some reason, God did not choose that for me or for our family. I am still working on learning how to stop looking *around* and to keep looking *up*.

2 Corinthians 10:12b - …*but they measuring themselves by themselves, and comparing themselves among themselves, are not wise.*

I do understand that just because I can not receive the same level of help that my friends do, does not mean that my children will be forgotten. Kevin's parents are wonderful grandparents. When they are in town, my three-year old loves every single minute he can spend with them. When they are away, they talk to him almost daily via phone or watch him play by means of "Skype." I am blessed by their constant involvement and how much can be learned from them. Likewise, my parents have certainly done the very best they can from a distance. They love talking with Channing on the phone, and they send little notes and gifts way more than they need to. When they do visit, they spoil him incredibly. Best of all, our children will have two parents, who love them deeply and adore spending time with them. We should feel honored to be the major influence in their lives, and to be able to spend so much uninterrupted time with them. God's plan for our children's lives will be perfect. Who am I to question the process?

Recently, I was blessed to hear our pastor deliver a wonderful sermon, at our church, which gave me the answer to all of the obstacles I was facing or could ever possibly face in the future – "Lordship." Lordship brings peace in all areas of life. When we come to the point when we *truly* believe that what God *does* in our lives and *allows* in our lives is for our ultimate good, we will have freedom from fear, anger, bitterness, and even questioning. As difficult as it is for us as humans to understand, maybe, in God's master-plan, the death of a child is not really a "bad" thing. In the same way, maybe the complications that we face are not "barriers," but rather "stepping stones" on the path to blessings. If God is actually the LORD of my life, and I am surrendered *completely* to His will, everything that happens to me is only "good" in the light of eternity. Often times, faith is truly blind, and sometimes, "God's glory" truly is our *only* answer to "why?"

2 Corinthians 5:7 - For we walk by faith, not by sight.

A ll I ever wanted was to be a mother. In August of 2000, I became pregnant with a precious little boy named "Cameron." At 19 weeks, I started having pains and leaking fluid. It was my first pregnancy, so I wasn't sure what was going on. I was ignorant to the fact that you could lose a baby that far along into a pregnancy. I called my doctor's office, and the nurse told me that I was just having Braxton-hicks contractions, and probably leaking urine. She said not to worry about it. As the pains got worse, I got scared, and called them back. This time, a doctor talked to me and told me to get to labor and delivery at the hospital immediately. I almost gave birth in the car. My precious son was stillborn, soon after arriving at the hospital. I was so angry. Why would this happen to me, when all I ever wanted was to be a mother? It is all I have ever dreamed about, and here I was, lying in a hospital bed, holding my lifeless son and saying "goodbye." I was mad at God. I cried out to Him, "How could you do this to me? What did I do to deserve this, while women who don't want babies just keep popping them out?" This was the moment that I began questioning God, for the first time in my life. I questioned Him for about a year, and then, I started feeling guilty for questioning Him. I asked God for His forgiveness, all the time. I began going back to church to worship, and I knew that I was right where I belonged.

In 2003, I found out that I was pregnant again. This time, the doctors were extra careful with me. I had a vaginal cerclage placed at only 11 weeks, and was put on hospital bed-rest for the remainder of my pregnancy. I just knew in my heart that this time, I was going to bring my baby home with me. On August 1, 2003 my water broke at 23 weeks, and I gave birth to yet another still-born son. We named him "Cameron Noah" (I call him Noah). This time hurt just as bad as the first time, and again I questioned God – "WHY?!?!?" Why had I felt so good about this? I was in the hospital, being taken care of around the clock. I had prayed every day, thanking God for allowing me to be taken care of this way and for allowing me to be pregnant again. All of this, only to lose another child? I almost felt like God was tormenting me on purpose; although, I knew in my heart that God would never do that.

As the days and months went on, the pain did not subside. Then, to add to the hurt, I found out that my husband had had an affair, while I was in the hospital on bed-rest. I asked God, "How much more can I take?" But, then, one day while I was visiting my sons at the cemetery, I began talking to God. It was on that day that my heart felt normal once again. I felt that I could love again. It was that day that I felt God answer my prayers. I realized that God was saying to me, "I love you, and I don't want to hurt you. One day, you will see your sons again. I picked YOU to help other women. I picked you to be the mother of these boys - out of every other woman in the world that I could have chosen. I picked YOUR SONS to be lucky enough to come straight to me, and to live in my kingdom in pure happiness - to never, ever hurt, be sick, etc. in their lives. I picked YOU for them to love and to wait for - to spend eternity with one day. In the meantime, you have to believe in me and to trust me, in order for that to happen."

I also realized that my walk with the Lord had not been as strong as it once was, and sometimes, these things have to happen in our lives to make our walk with him closer once again. I knew that God should always come first in our lives, and He had not been coming first in my life. God loved me so much that He made something drastic happen in my life. He wanted to draw me closer to Himself again, because He wants me to live eternally with Him that much. I was lost and then, this happened, and God found me, protected me, and SAVED me. I realized that this wasn't about my sons, but it was about ME, my future, and what could happen to me, if I didn't get my relationship with the Lord back. Losing my sons will never stop hurting, and the pain will never go away, but it has helped tremendously in my life. It has made me a stronger person, it has made me love the Lord more than I ever have, it has made me appreciate the simple things in life (when I once didn't), and it has made me realize what is *really* important and what isn't. It made me realize that I need to have faith in God. He loves us, even when bad things happen.

In 2006, when my faith in the Lord was stronger than ever, He led me to do research on my condition. I found out that I could have an abdominal cerclage placed and have a great chance of delivering a healthy child. (This is something my doctors never told me about.) I approached a team of doctors with my idea. At first, they refused to place it, but the Lord gave me the words that I needed to convince these doctors to place it. On Feb. 1, 2006, I had my cerclage placed, pre-pregnancy. In July 2007, I found out I was pregnant once again.

During my pregnancy, my husband finally left me for his mistress. I could handle it, with God's strong hands around me, comforting me. I went all the way to 26 weeks, without having to be on bed-rest. At 26 weeks, I was put on bed-rest at home. Then, at 34 weeks, my water broke, and I gave birth via c-section to the most stinkin' cute little boy you have ever seen! His name is "Garrett Noah," and he is the love of my life. He looks just like his brothers, and every time I look at him, I smile and say "Thank you, God. Thank you for this angel of mine. Thank you for everything that I went through to have him. Thank you for allowing me to see his brothers in him."

Now, I can even say, "Thank you for allowing my husband to leave." There is a reason for all of this. Garrett and I are better off without him. When Garrett was 2, I met a wonderful man, who is now a part of our lives. He loves Garrett, just like his own, and Garrett loves him. We are planning on getting married next year. I now have my perfect family. It may not seem perfect to some people, but it is the perfect life that God planned out for me, when He created me.

Sonya Luddy
Belmont, North Carolina

W e had been married for only five months, but it already seemed we had been waiting a lifetime to have a baby. With both of us coming from big families, children of our own were very important to us. So we were thrilled to find out we were finally expecting. We began talking about names and attending doctor's appointments. I felt a little silly, this being our first child, that I, being a petite person, was becoming so large so soon. But halfway through the pregnancy, an ultrasound confirmed what my mom had already quietly suspected but what we had never dreamed of— we were expecting twins, both boys. We were ecstatic and a bit overwhelmed.

For two months, we planned, it seemed, in a dream. We decided on a 2nd boy's name and talked about how we would accommodate two. People gave some early gifts: matching sleepers, a second crib, a second bouncy chair, and a second infant car seat. We had to change doctors because we had been planning a home birth, and our doctor would not deliver twins at home. We were also moved in status to a high-risk pregnancy, with more frequent check-ups.

At 30 weeks, with just a couple of weeks before the baby shower given by our church where we were to be blessed with the generous gift of a double stroller, we were off to see the high-risk doctor for the first time. We were very excited to see a 2nd ultrasound of our little guys and see how much they had grown. The technician did a quick sweep over "Baby A" (Ezra Augustine) and began to evaluate "Baby B" (Ethan Patrick). She gave us a glowing evaluation of "Baby B" and then, in very general terms, said that she was concerned about the lack of growth progress in "Baby A," and that she was going to go get the doctor to talk with us. I lay there in a daze, trying to wrap my mind around what all of this might mean, and looking at my husband almost as if to say, "Please tell me this isn't what it sounds like!"

The doctor came in and explained to us that there had been a "demise" of "Baby A;" or simply, that he was no longer living. They could not say why he had died or even how long he had been dead. I would need to continue carrying him until I was able to give birth to the other baby.

We left the office with everyone's most sincere condolences, and we walked out to our car feeling that dull, numbing ache that is somehow still so intense. I've always remembered since then how perfectly beautiful that sunny October 6 was, a seeming direct contradiction to the darkness and heaviness of our sorrow. But as we arrived home and cried for hours in each other's arms, talking when various thoughts came to our minds, and reading the promises of Scripture, the comfort that God promises His people poured over our aching hearts like the warming sunshine of that autumn day.

We were buoyed up by the remembrance of the great love that God has for His people, as a loving Father, one who does *all* things perfectly, and does not ever afflict His beloved ones needlessly. We were comforted by the thought that God who created our little Ezra in each part and planned for every moment of his life and breath, knew before the beginning of the world exactly how long his little life would be. His purpose for the little son that we would never get to know or feed or teach was unknown to us, and yet bigger than our understanding. Somehow, in those hours, and the many days following, He gave us the ability to trust that He knew best for the small life that was no longer ours on this earth, and that He knew best for our own lives as well. And we, of course, felt so blessed that we had still been spared our other little boy.

This does not mean that I did not have moments of confusion or anxiety over the next few weeks.

On the drive home from the ultrasound that day, I thought of the baby's room we had already set up for two: two cribs with blankets and individual stuffed animals. Upon walking into our house, my husband immediately shut the door to the room; It's hard to say which was more painful, to look on the extra crib, thinking how it would not be needed now or to pass by the room with the door closed. I would take my daily walk praising the Lord for His goodness and for sparing one child, and yet sobbing with my hand on my belly, "Please don't take this one!"

I tried not to think about the fact that I was carrying a dead baby and fought terror over losing the baby that was still alive. I both lived for and dreaded the weekly non-stress tests, always afraid that when I went in, they would find no movement or heartbeat. Even these moments of fear, though, were countered by the Holy Spirit reminding me of God's love and faithfulness and mercy, that the Lord *had* spared the life of the surviving twin this far and that his life was in the hands of the One who gives *and* takes away [**Job 1:20**].

We were now also facing the need to have a C-section, while we had been hoping for a natural birth, since the deceased twin was blocking the way to the birth canal. This disappointment and apprehension, too, seemed to be amazingly quieted by the Lord. Things continued to check out fine medically over the next three weeks. Then two days before I hit the 33-week mark, I began showing signs of labor. Once in the hospital, the doctors attempted to stop the labor, while at the same time determining that I should be given steroid shots to try to develop the baby's lungs as much as possible in case delivery proved to be unavoidable. We were transferred to a hospital that had greater capabilities for high-risk deliveries and NICU facilities.

I was very upset that I should be going into labor so early, and going through the experience of contractions for the first time did nothing to settle me. But the Lord continued to keep our hearts upon Him and His promises as we whirled through the blur of those 38 hours or so of uncertainty. Though the doctors were able to postpone the labor for a while, it was soon apparent that it was the Lord's will that these babies be delivered sooner than later.

Around 2:20 a.m., on October 30, 2004, a very still and quiet Ezra Augustine, weighing only 12 ounces, was delivered by C-section, followed by a feisty little Ethan Patrick, weighing 3 pounds and 13 ounces. In the fog of the spinal medication, I still listened intently for that newborn cry. Though it seemed like an eternity, we finally heard it, and I cried. I saw him briefly out of the corner of my eye, then he was whisked away to the NICU, and I to recovery.

When I was back in my room with my husband at my side, they brought us Ezra. I will treasure and probably replay those precious few moments in my mind as long as I have memory. It was not the disturbing experience I expected it to be. Wrapped in a blanket, though very still, the little body I held in my arms was my sweet, little son. His tiny face looked deep in sleep. I have missed holding him many times since then, but I'm so glad we were given the opportunity for those few minutes. It was dear and healing.

We also had the great blessing of a beautiful funeral one week later. Surrounded by our closest family members and our pastor, we sang hymns and read Scripture that reminded us of the blessing of Ezra's short life and the promise we have in Christ of the resurrection. It was another beautiful fall day, more chilly than it had been just weeks before but refreshing somehow too. Even as we were surrounded that day by the fallen leaves and had the reality of the separation of death before us, we had just as much reality of the promise of new life beyond the winter of our mourning.

We left the cemetery that day and drove straight to the NICU to visit our living son who was struggling valiantly to gain strength. Each day, we watched the Lord give him appetite, weight gain, strength, and finally the ability to breathe steadily with no monitoring. After just 17 days in the NICU care, we were able to bring him home with us. To date, the Lord has blessed us with the care and blessing of this adventure of a boy for almost 7 years now. We realize more and more the gravity of the responsibility with which God entrusted us on that October day.

We have never discovered the cause of Ezra's death. Ethan has grown up being told the story of the brother he has never known. The older he gets, the more capable he is of realizing God's preservation of his own life. He knows that God had a particular purpose for sparing his own life, as doctors were concerned for a time that something harmful could have been passed over from Ezra to him. He sometimes talks of what it would be like to have a brother totally identical to him to play with, study with, and talk to. I often think of it myself. Though the loss is felt differently over time, the place Ezra first held in my heart will never be filled by anything else. There will always, I think, be tenderness and always an ache when I think of him and of all the things we didn't get to share with him. But just as enduring will be the confidence that God does *all things well*. This has been the greatest comfort in our loss. Whatever may seem "unfair" to us as we look with our limited human perspective at a world which suffers under the curse of sin, must certainly be part of the "all things beautiful," that all things are done for our good and His glory. In this, we can bless Him, even in our loss, and praise Him that He counted us part of His beautiful plan.

I end with the hymn that was one of my rocks during our loss of Ezra and many times since:

Whate'er My God Ordains Is Right
Samuel Rodigast, 1675
Whate'er my God ordains is right,
Holy His will abideth.
I will be still whate'er He does,
and follow where He guideth.
He is my God, though dark my road.
He holds me that I shall not fall.
Wherefore to Him I leave it all.
Whate'er my God ordains is right.
He never will deceive me.
He leads me by the proper path;
I know He will not leave me,
I take, content, what He hath sent.
His hand can turn my griefs away.
And patiently I wait His day.
Whate'er my God ordains is right,
Though now this cup in drinking,
May bitter seem to my faint heart,
I take it all unshrinking.
My God is true, each morn anew.
Sweet comfort yet shall fill my heart,
And pain and sorrow shall depart.
Whate'er my God ordains is right,
Here shall my stand be taken.
Though sorrow, need, or death be mine,
Yet I am not forsaken.
My Father's care is round me there;

He holds me that I shall not fall.
And so to Him I leave it all.

Rebekah Lindstrom
Rolling Meadows, Illinois

Chapter 9

The Miracle of a Blessed Future

Each time I laid on that table to "visit" with my fourth baby, by way of ultrasound, I wiped away tears of joy. I would never take the sound of a heartbeat for granted again. For a short time during my second trimester, my pregnancy became a bit easier. The sickness subsided and, eventually, went into a short "remission." Every kick and every movement inside my womb was reassurance that I had another day with my little miracle. God used the losses in my life to change me significantly during this time. I learned so very much - things that I never could have learned any other way. My attitude adjustments had gone a long way in making difficult days much more bearable and good days that much more exciting. I found great joy in preparing for a new little one to join our household.

Then...along came the third trimester, and with it a whole new set of challenges – mostly physical – which tried to conquer my "new-found" spirit of peace and joy. By this time, I was *huge*! I don't mean "beach ball" huge, I'm talking "exercise ball" huge. My doctor said I was carrying extra fluid, and my extra weight was all in the front. My little "Baby Joy" would be free to keep up his extreme regiment of "joyful" gymnastics, right up until the moment he entered the world. What a thrill that must have been for him. Meanwhile, I had a slight glimpse of what "Humpty-

Dumpty" may have felt like, had he ever walked out of the children's rhyme and into real life. Although we could laugh about it later, these facts contributed to my pain increasing dramatically and, along with it, my discouragement. I was more than ready to meet my little boy. By this time, I had been pregnant for a little over a year, and I was tired, to put it mildly. Only God's amazing grace allowed me to press on each day. When my doctor, finally, recommended full bed-rest, I could only picture my miniature "Tasmanian devil" (in disguise as a three year old, blue-eyed angel) zipping around the house, unattended, and wreaking havoc on everything in his path. I couldn't help but laugh. Once again, though, God's ways were above my understanding. My Mother-in-law, upon hearing the seeming "joke of the day," offered to watch Channing every day for me, until the birth of the baby. Words? I had none. I was *beyond* appreciative! It seemed way too much to ask of *anyone*, especially knowing how incredibly full of energy my little man was. On the other hand, I was so disappointed that my time, one-on-one with him, was going to be over, just like that. It was not easy to kiss him "good-bye" each morning, and I felt guilty about my inability to take care of him, but I was relieved to know that he was being loved and well-cared for. It was a gift that I could never repay.

Seeing a "light at the end of the tunnel" definitely made entering those final months easier - mentally and emotionally. However, during this time, I began feeling very strongly, for many of the reasons already mentioned, that I didn't want to go through a pregnancy *ever again*! I knew that this decision was a big one, and carried a lot of responsibility with it. I recognized that there were so many women who would *love* to carry a child, and that they may find this inconceivable and maybe selfish. I understood that my friends, family, and especially my husband, may not completely agree with me. So, I had to take time to consider these things in depth, and pray for wisdom and discretion. There were several things that I felt could help make this decision easier and hopefully clearer - for myself and those around me.

First of all, I needed to remember that it is possible that another pregnancy would not be in the best interest for my overall health. This is a *major* factor for me. Each person has their *own* limitations, and each person has to determine what is feasible for themselves. No one, not even a doctor, can tell you what *your* true limitations are. Actually, several of the doctors/surgeons that I saw, did tell me that everyone's body handles pain differently. I could have the exact same disease as the next person, but my body could react completely differently to it than does another person's body. The pain that I faced during this fourth pregnancy, due to my spinal condition, was nearly intolerable at times. By the end of my eighth month, just getting out of bed to use the bathroom could only happen by strong-will and a lot of prayer. (And of course, the frightful thought of how much effort it would take to change wet sheets!) During the entire pregnancy, I struggled with muscle spasms, which did not even allow me to stand up straight most of the time, not to mention play on the floor with my son, get him dressed, or help him in and out of the bathtub. Each pregnancy has the potential to further damage my mobility. I desperately want to not only have babies, but also to be able to take care of them. Some women cannot have children because their reproductive systems are incapable of functioning properly. Many other women cannot have children for other health reasons. The ability to have a child is much more than just being able to conceive. A woman's body must be strong enough to carry that child to term, and then to rear that child for the next 18+ years. I struggled with guilt for not wanting to "try harder," but in my heart, I knew that the idea was just not promising. As the time passes, maybe something will change my mind, or I will gain the necessary strength, but either way, I feel that I need to be a good steward of the body God has entrusted to me for this lifetime.

Another important area, I must consider, follows along the same line of thought. I need to regard the desires of those in authority over me. As a Christian, I need to obey God. God always wants the very best for my life. He knows my limitations. He will never ask me to do anything that is beyond my ability, without giving me the strength that I will need to do it. This may mean that He will ask me to do something that I do not want to do or feel able to do. I must be prepared to obey Him, by keeping my mind and heart open. I know that I will always be the happiest within His will. I do not want to miss out on a blessing that He has planned for me because of a hard or rebellious spirit. It is often during the times that He "stretches" us, that we grow the most.

On the same token, as a wife, I need to submit to my husband. My husband undoubtedly has his own ideas and desires in the area of growing our family. I must be willing to listen to what he feels is important and necessary for our future. On the other hand, as a Godly husband, he should also be willing to listen and to think about what *I* have to say. He cannot possibly know the extent of my pain or the impact of it upon my daily life. I have found that I need to pray that God will help me show my husband where I lack and where I need help, and that He will give him the patience, support, and compassion that I need from him.

Ephesians 5:21-24 - Submitting yourselves one to another in the fear of God. Wives, submit yourselves unto your own husbands, as unto the Lord. For the husband is the head of the wife, even as Christ is the head of the church: and he is the saviour of the body. Therefore as the church is subject unto Christ, so let the wives be to their own husbands in every thing.

I need to remember to communicate with my husband, as he cannot read my mind. What's more, I have to share my burdens with him, and I have to ask for his support, when I need it. Sometimes, I find that this is very humbling for me. I have always been so self-sufficient, and to ask for help means that I am giving up an element of my independence. I have come to believe that, like the Apostle Paul, maybe, God has chosen to give me a "thorn in the flesh," by way of 24/7 pain. If I am totally honest, I *need* this "thorn" in my life. I have always struggled with the area of pride in accomplishment. God uses my pain, daily, to remind me that He gave me *all* of my abilities, He enables me to use them, and that *He alone* deserves the glory for what is accomplished in my life.

As difficult as it is, I must also learn to share my feelings regarding my limitations in childbearing/rearing with my husband. If I have the proper attitude, and if I cover the conversation in prayer, I should be able to convey my inner feelings and desires with him in a Godly manner. If my husband is following Christ's example, and loving me as Christ loves the church, He will be willing to consider my requests and concerns, and we should be able to work out a solution that we can both be comfortable and content with.

Ephesians 5: 25,28-31 - Husbands, love your wives, even as Christ also loved the church, and gave himself for it;...So ought men to love their wives as their own bodies. He that loveth his wife loveth himself. For no man ever yet hated his own flesh; but nourisheth and cherisheth it, even as the Lord the church: For we are members of his body, of his flesh, and of his bones. For this cause shall a man leave his father and mother, and shall be joined unto his wife, and they two shall be one flesh.

There are also several other options to consider when pregnancy is not logical, safe, recommended or possible. Giving birth is not the only way to "parent" a child. Before the beginning of time, God designed each family, and determined who would be a part of each of them. He knows the children who are to be born, and what family He designed them for. Just because a child is born to a particular mother and father, does not mean that that child belongs with those individuals for the duration of his/her life. God has hand-picked each of our children - and in the light of eternity - maternity and paternity, family trees, and genealogies really do not mean much of anything.

> **Jeremiah 1:5a** - *Before I formed thee in the belly I knew thee; and before thou camest forth out of the womb I sanctified thee…*

Foster parenting and adoption are such wonderful alternatives. What a blessing to take a child from a life of uncertainty and/or abuse, and bring them up in the knowledge of Christ and His love. What a beautiful picture of what our Savior did for us, when He saved us from our sins by His death on the cross. What if God had refused to consider any child that wasn't "biological?" Where would *we* be? I would love to share this truth in a very tangible way with my biological children, by teaching them to love others and to be accepting of those who are not from the same background or "mold" that we are accustomed to. (I am not talking about being tolerant of sin or of those, whose lifestyle is in rebellion to God.) I want my children to understand how very blessed they are, and that if it were not for the grace and mercy of an all-powerful God, they could be in entirely different circumstances.

Romans 12:3 - For I say, through the grace given unto me, to every man that is among you, not to think of himself more highly than he ought to think; but to think soberly, according as God hath dealt to every man the measure of faith.

Certainly, each one of these options calls for serious deliberation, and each one comes with its own set of responsibilities and complications. However, God will certainly provide a way and the means, if His plan leads in one of these directions.

Other ways of becoming a "parent," without the same level of long-term commitment that comes with adoption or foster parenting, could include: a career in childcare, special education, teaching, becoming an "aunt" to a child with little or no extended family, a "mother's aide" to help a young or inexperienced mom, or even mentoring a child who needs some extra counsel and attention. We do not have many relatives living near us. Our children may not have the opportunity to ever really know their aunts, uncles, or cousins very well. We have found that our friends from church have become our "family," and our son calls them "aunts" and "uncles." Some are opposed to this concept, and feel this confuses children. Certainly, this is something you have to decide for your own family, and it usually depends upon the accessibility of biological relatives in your lives. We truly believe that for us, friends have filled the void that family fills for others. We are blessed to have the influence of both of our children's grandparents in their lives, even if it is from a distance. Children are intelligent, and as they grow up, they will come to understand the difference between blood relatives and "adopted" relatives. In this evil and deceptive world that we live in, the more guidance, love and protection we can allow for our children, the better it will be for them – physically and spiritually.

I have often had the opportunity to be a "parent" in one of the above mentioned areas. I have taught, been a nanny, mentored, and worked in childcare for many years. It is such a blessing to be a positive influence in a child's life, especially for a child who might otherwise be lonely or neglected. God has placed a special desire in my heart to minister to women – especially those who are struggling and hurting. I have written, compiled, and taught quite a bit of material for teenage girls, and am currently working on a degree in Biblical Counseling. I have found that God will often use me only if and when I am ready to be used. I went from accepting the fact that I might never be a mother, to becoming a mother to four children of my own, as well as becoming a parent-figure to other people's children. I have been blessed beyond measure, and God has seen fit to fill my once-empty cup to overflowing.

> *Joel 2:25a* - *And I will restore to you the years that the locust hath eaten...*

> *Isaiah 61:3* - *To appoint unto them that mourn in Zion, to give unto them beauty for ashes, the oil of joy for mourning, the garment of praise for the spirit of heaviness; that they might be called trees of righteousness, the planting of the LORD, that he might be glorified.*

The true miracle of a blessed future is played out in two major parts: Ours and God's. We need to prepare *ourselves* – through study, prayer, and counsel – to be ready to "live out" our desires, should God fulfill them. Praying for God to send you a husband does not make you a good wife, in the same way that praying for God to bless you with a child does not make you a good mother. If you want to be a mom, then work at preparing to be the best mom that you can be *now*, and trust God to give you a child in *His* timing. There are so many things that I wish I had known and learned about marriage, before I got married over a decade ago, and I know that in another 10 years, I will have learned so much more. In the same way, I am working extra hard to extend my knowledge in the area of parenting. I want to learn as much as possible, before I get too far down this tricky road of motherhood. God will only give us what we can handle. I want to be capable of handling the "desires of my heart."

God's part in a blessed future is the most necessary component. I must remember that no matter what happens in my life, *God* is always God and *I* am not. He needs to be the LORD of my life, in *every* area – not just the uncomplicated ones. God is truly worthy of our obedience and our service. He had given us so much, and has promised us so much:

- Hope and a future:

Jeremiah 29:11(NIV 2011) - For I know the plans I have for you," declares the LORD, "plans to prosper you and not to harm you, plans to give you hope and a future.

- Help and strength:

Isaiah 41:10 - Fear thou not; for I am with thee: be not dismayed; for I am thy God: I will strengthen thee; yea, I will help thee; yea, I will uphold thee with the right hand of my righteousness.

- To give us everything that is *best* for us:

Psalm 84:11 - For the LORD God is a sun and shield: the LORD will give grace and glory: no good thing will he withhold from them that walk uprightly.

- To work out everything for our good and His glory:

Romans 8:28 - *And we know that all things work together for good to them that love God, to them who are the called according to his purpose.*

Isaiah 48:11 - *For mine own sake, even for mine own sake, will I do it: for how should my name be polluted? and I will not give my glory unto another.*

God is, beyond doubt, a perfect Father. I have to continually remind myself of the truth that if there were an easier, better, or more painless way of accomplishing His will in my life, He would certainly do it. He loved me enough to send His *only* Son to suffer in this evil world and die at the hands of His own creation. Jesus was nailed to a cross made from a tree that He formed with His own hands. He grew the very thorns that pierced His brow. He *chose* to die in order to pay the penalty for our sins and to make a way for us to have a relationship with the Holy God of Heaven. If God can love us that much for eternity's sake, surely He must want to give us wonderful blessings in our present daily lives as well. Trusting God to not only direct and control our lives, but also to bring what He knows is best for us at the very best time is the key to joyful and content living.

Psalm 127:3, "Children are a gift of the Lord."

In my life, so far, God has gifted me with two little boys, ages 5 and 2. I love them dearly. My husband and I felt that our family was not yet complete. We really wanted a little girl so we read books, prayed a lot, and even bought a few hair bows as an act of faith. God was good; life was good. I remember lying on the ultrasound table and hearing the words, "It's a girl," as tears ran down my face. We were finally getting our little girl! I was 17 weeks at my next ultrasound and everything looked well. We named her "Aubrieana Lashay." We scheduled an appointment for the main ultrasound, at 21 weeks. I asked my mother if she wanted to go with me to my appointment, have lunch, and go buy some "girlie" baby clothes. As I was lying on the table, Aubrieana looked like she was waving, and her mouth was wide open. We joked that she was going to like to sing, just like I do.

The nurse began asking weird questions: "Have you had any pressure?" "Felt any different?" "So, no pressure at all?" I knew something must be wrong. She said the baby looked fine and the doctor would see us in a few minutes. I didn't have to wait very long before I heard my name called. When the nurse took me to the room, she gave me a gown and said the doctor wanted to examine me. I thought that was weird on my 21-week visit. When the doctor came in, she asked me how I was feeling. I told her the normal stuff like tired, back hurts, etc. Then, it was her turn to talk, and what she had to say, shook my whole world. She told me I would need to leave the office and go straight to the hospital. My cervix was short. It should have been at the very least 2cm; mine was 0.6cm. I would need to have a rescue cerclage. She checked me out and told me I was dilated to 3cm. I got dressed and walked out to the waiting room trying not to cry. It didn't work; the tears were streaming down my face. I walked over to my mother who was trying to keep my boys from being too loud. She looked up and knew something was wrong. We got all the paperwork we needed and headed straight to the hospital.

For the next 24 hours, they had me in a bed tilted up at the end, so that my feet were slightly above my head, trying to move my cervix up a little. The next morning, they took me to surgery and put in the cerclage. Everything went really well. They thought that I had bacterial vaginosis, so they started me on some strong antibiotics. I was in the hospital for 5 days. Finally, I was able to go home, but I had to stay on strict bed-rest.

I was only home one night before my world went from being "shaken" to a full-blown "earthquake." I began having some unusual discharge. So I got my husband to take me to the hospital. They checked me, and because the doctor thought it was still from the bacterial vaginosis, she sent me back home. That was at 9pm. By 1am, I was awake with contractions every 5 minutes and the discharge was worse. I called my mother and she rushed me back to the hospital. They admitted me to a room. I had spiked a fever of 103°, and the contractions kept getting stronger. They couldn't get them to stop. The nurses could not get the machine to pick up the contractions, so they did not know how often or hard they were coming. At 1pm, they sent me for an ultrasound, to have my cerclage checked. While the doctor was doing the ultrasound, she told my mother that I was having full blown contractions. I was moaning and praying with each one. The high risk doctor wanted to examine me and look at my amniotic fluid. He drew the fluid and it had a greenish tint. When he examined me, he realized how serious this was. I was rushed to the delivery room. Nothing could be done. Our baby girl was coming into the world way too early. This could not be happening! So many thoughts and questions were going through my mind. At 6:58pm, Aubrieana was born. She lived for an hour. During that hour, we got to hold her and tell her "goodbye." It all seemed like a nightmare. I kept thinking, "This can't be real; I have to wake up!" Suddenly, we weren't celebrating a birth; we were planning a funeral. This was wrong on so many levels.

When I was finally released from the hospital, we went straight to the store to find our daughter something to wear for her funeral. She was so tiny, 1lb 1oz and 11 inches long. We had to buy a baby-doll outfit for her. I also wanted something for her head, so I bought what I needed to make her a head band. She would never be able to wear the one that I had already bought for her. Then, we headed to the funeral home to make arrangements. The next few days were a blur of people saying they were "so sorry," etc. It was the day after we buried her that it all became real - the pain hit me like a bullet. Life was not good and dare I say, dare I think that even God was not good? I was so angry! How could God do this to us! We go to church. We live "right." We don't drink, smoke, or even cuss. Why? Why? Why? Those first few weeks, it seemed like I wouldn't be able to survive. The tears flowed like a river. I remember begging God to please just tell me, "why?" Why couldn't He just send me a dream or some type of message?

As the weeks went by, the days got a little better, and a little easier. The tears slowed and things became "normal" again. It has been 2 months since we lost Aubrieana. I still miss her and always will, but I have found peace. I am no longer mad at God. I am thankful that He carried me through this awful time in my life. I have peace in knowing that Aubrieana is awaiting my homecoming in heaven. I've always known that heaven is real, but now, I have a longing that I can't explain. To have no pain, tears, or sorrow, to be with Jesus, and to see my little girl run and play and smile. Wow, what an awesome thought! I am reminded of John 3:16 and how God's Son had to die, so that I can live with Him in Heaven one day. I know God understands my pain. He has been there, and as I walk through this trial in my life, He guides me. I remember locking myself in my room and just crying out to God. I could feel His peace overtake me - the peace that passes all understanding. It's for sure that I don't understand this loss, but my faith in Him allows me to continue on the path that He has for me. He is my Jehovah-Rapha, the "God Who Heals." This path is a long one, full of anger, questions, jealousy, sadness, pain, etc. The list of emotions is endless. However, I also find joy, peace, patience, and all the "fruit of the Spirit," that I am promised in His Word, to nourish my body, soul and spirit. I am not walking alone; He is right beside me and when needed, He carries me.

Jeremiah 31:13, "I will turn their mourning into joy and will comfort them and give them joy for their sorrow."

Redina Rose Wilson
Union, South Carolina

-◦❊⊣ Chapter 10 ⊢❊◦-

The Miracle of Compassion

I was admitted into the hospital on September 23, 2010, after nearly two exhausting months on bed-rest, of which I remember very little besides being uncomfortable and cantankerous. Through God's amazing grace, I had a labor and delivery that was nothing short of miraculous. The anesthesiologist was extremely knowledgeable about spinal issues, and was comfortable with giving me the epidural. He even felt that it would be to my benefit, and much easier on my back. I only had about 45 minutes in the entire experience, when I had some minimal pain and, the anesthesiologist quickly realized that the medication calculation was inaccurate and increased the dosage. *I was pain-free for the first time in about seven years!* What an awesome blessing to be freed of my constant pain long enough to enjoy the birth of my child. My doctor was amazed when I broke into laughter, between "pushes." I was excited to have the opportunity to see the top of my son's head, just before he entered the world, thanks to a hand-mirror I had brought along for quick "touch-ups" right before those wonderful "I-just-delivered-a-baby photos." I could not stop a silly giggle from escaping my lips, at the sight of his wrinkled, raisin-like head, covered in dark hair. A couple of pushes later and our son, "Baby Joy", a.k.a. Carter Alan, was born at 3:15pm on September 24th, weighing 8lbs. 10oz. He was so beautiful!

As the doctor placed him on my chest, I began sobbing. What a journey this had been. God had, once again, seen fit to grant our request for a child to hold in our arms. In the days, weeks, months, and years ahead, there will be laughter and sorrow, good days and bad. My confidence and contentment is found in the One who never changes. I am learning to rest completely secure in His arms – with joy – even in the times of mourning.

As I bring my story to a close, I would like to offer a few challenges. First of all, to those of you who have been blessed to have never had to experience these painful circumstances in your life, I would urge you to seek out those who are hurting around you. Please, do not allow yourself to be blind to the pain that others are experiencing, and do not be afraid to speak to them. Chances are, many of the women in your life have been touched by the loss of a child. Most have never had an opportunity to address and to deal with this grief, and most likely, they would welcome the opportunity to talk about it. All moms want to brag about their babies, even the ones, who are now in heaven. Allow God to use you to bless and to comfort them in a time of need. Take them a meal, offer to watch their other children for a few hours, or just share a prayer and a hug. Maybe you just need to weep with them. I hope these stories have inspired in you – as they have in me – a heart for grieving mothers.

Romans 12:15 - Rejoice with them that do rejoice, and weep with them that weep.

Second, I would like to encourage those of you who are presently dealing with the pain of a loss through a miscarriage, a stillbirth, an abortion, or the death of a child in some other way to seek out people to share your story with. For some of us, this is easy - For others, not so much. Either way, talking through the pain allows you to not only hear your thoughts out loud, which often sheds a new light on them, but also allows those around you to minister to you and to help you. Allow God to speak to you through others and to restore your broken heart. Then, likewise, use your experience to minister to others. God often uses pain to bring us peace. If we never had to go through the hard times, we would never know the wondrous and unending grace of God. Christ is our solid rock and a secure shelter during the storms of life. He promises to hold us in His hand and never let us go:

> **John 10:28-29** - *And I give unto them eternal life; and they shall never perish, neither shall any man pluck them out of my hand. My Father, which gave them me, is greater than all; and no man is able to pluck them out of my Father's hand.*

He even keeps track of all of our tears:

> **Psalm 56:8b** - *... put thou my tears into thy bottle: are they not in thy book?*

Surely, a God who cares about the number of tears that we shed must also, beyond a doubt, care about *all* of our feelings. What an amazing thought! What an amazing God!

Lastly, for those of you who do not know Christ as the Savior and LORD of your life, I plead with you to seek Him, before it is too late.

> **Isaiah 55:6** - *Seek ye the LORD while he may be found, call ye upon him while he is near.*

God understands the loss of a child. He *chose* to give up His only Son for the weak, helpless, and sinful creatures that He created. He watched the human race defiantly ignore Him and decide to live life by their own selfish standards.

He watched as His creation shook its fist in His face, and laughed at righteousness and truth.

> **Romans 3:12** - *They are all gone out of the way, they are together become unprofitable; there is none that doeth good, no, not one.*

> **Romans 3:23** - *For all have sinned, and come short of the glory of God.*

And even though He could have easily chosen to destroy us, He chose to save us instead. Because sin cannot be tolerated by a holy and just God, payment had to be made. The punishment for sin was death and separation from God.

> **Romans 6:23a** - For the wages of sin is death...

This meant eternal damnation in hell for anyone who fell short of His *perfect* standard. No matter how "good" you believe that you are, if you have been guilty of *one* sin, you are guilty of them *all*. God had compassion upon us and allowed His *only* child – holy, perfect, and completely without sin – to come to this evil world, in the form of human flesh, in order to be the ultimate sacrifice for all sin.

> **Romans 6:23b** - *...but the gift of God is eternal life through Jesus Christ our Lord.*

> **Philippians 2:7-8** - *But made himself of no reputation, and took upon him the form of a servant, and was made in the likeness of men: And being found in fashion as a man, he humbled himself, and became obedient unto death, even the death of the cross.*

What an amazing sacrifice! This holy child was entrusted to a young woman, a mom – just as sinful and unworthy as the rest of us – to be cared for. Jesus was mocked, hated, and even homeless for most of his earthly life, and ultimately was "sold out" by one of His own followers to face a grueling death. He was nailed to a cross – crafted from a tree, which He created – and He was hung there for the entire world to scoff at. Yet, as He died, He thought of you and me, and forgave us with His last breath. The cross and the blood that He shed upon it became the bridge that can connect us to a holy God.

Romans 5:8 - But God commendeth his love toward us, in that, while we were yet sinners, Christ died for us.

Ephesians 2:13-14,18 - But now in Christ Jesus ye who sometimes were far off are made nigh by the blood of Christ. For he is our peace, who hath made both one, and hath broken down the middle wall of partition between us...For through him we both have access by one Spirit unto the Father.

Colossians 1:13-14 - Who hath delivered us from the power of darkness, and hath translated us into the kingdom of his dear Son: In whom we have redemption through his blood, even the forgiveness of sins.

What a humbling thought. He knew all about you and me – including every single action, intention, and thought of our hearts, souls, and minds. He designed each of us before the world began. He knew every feature, every detail, and even the number of hairs on our heads. He knew that we would continually sin, that we would reject Him over and over again, and that many would hate Him, but He chose to love us and to give Himself for us anyway. As He rose

191

from the grave on that blessed day, He conquered death, sin, and hell - for you and for me. The only thing that He asks in return is for us to confess and repent of our sin, to accept His payment for it, and to allow Him to be Lord of our lives. He wants the dominion in our hearts, souls, and minds.

Romans 10:13 - For whosoever shall call upon the name of the Lord shall be saved.

John 1:12 - But as many as received him, to them gave he power to become the sons of God, even to them that believe on his name.

Salvation from sin and death was certainly not free, but it was paid for us by Christ. If you have never asked Jesus to come into your life and to free you from the bondage of the devil and his lies, to give you eternal life, and to rule and reign in your heart and life, I beg you to do it now!

Romans 10:9-10 - That if thou shalt confess with thy mouth the Lord Jesus, and shalt believe in thine heart that God hath raised him from the dead, thou shalt be saved. For with the heart man believeth unto righteousness; and with the mouth confession is made unto salvation.

Acts 26:18 - To open their eyes, and to turn them from darkness to light, and from the power of Satan unto God, that they may receive forgiveness of sins, and inheritance among them which are sanctified by faith that is in me.

Only God knows the length of our days, and the number of opportunities we will be given to accept Him. If God is calling you, seek out someone you feel comfortable talking to, contact me via email at joycomeswiththemourning@hotmail.com, or send me a message through Facebook, on the "Joy Comes with the Mourning" book page. (On this page, you may also connect with others, who are going through similar circumstances.) I would be thrilled to explain this amazing gift to you in further detail or to answer any questions you may have. If you would like to read the entire account of Jesus for yourself, I would suggest you begin in the Bible with the Gospel of John in the New Testament. Please, do not wait until it is too late. The time to answer God is *now*.

II Corinthians 6:2 - For he saith, I have heard thee in a time accepted, and in the day of salvation have I succoured thee: behold, now is the accepted time; behold, now is the day of salvation.

In conclusion, every single life is truly a miracle. Every child is a gift from the hand of an omniscient and omnipotent God. Whether for a few months or for a lifetime, each moment with them is precious. Our children are not our own. They belong to the Creator, and they are only on loan to us for a season. It is not for us to know how long that may be. When this truth made its way from my head to my heart, my loss was much easier to accept as a blessing in disguise. I would encourage you to appreciate every moment that you are given, and not to waste time wishing for what you cannot have. If you have children in heaven, I encourage you to praise God for the wonderful opportunity to have had a child, and to thank Him for sparing them the pain and sin of this evil world. If you have children, whom you can hold in your arms, hold them with all the love you have in your heart for as long as you can. Do not waste a moment wishing for a "would-be" future. We need to be thankful for and learn from our past, hope and pray for our future, and live with contentment in our present. As one of my many life verses says:

> ***Philippians 4:11-13*** - *Not that I speak in respect of want: for I have learned, in whatsoever state I am, therewith to be content. I know both how to be abased, and I know how to abound: every where and in all things I am instructed both to be full and to be hungry, both to abound and to suffer need. I can do all things through Christ which strengtheneth me.*

Epilogue

"Bring it on!"

One detail that struck me, as I worked on editing this book for publishing, is the vast amount of unique circumstances that make up each individual testimony. I have literally read and heard dozens of stories from women, who have all experienced the loss of a child, and not one is the same in any way. We all have a distinctive set of life experiences and outside influences, which cause us to respond in different ways to a very similar event in our lives. We all grieve in our own way: some quietly, others loudly; some slowly, others quickly. I pray that this book has opened your eyes to the infinite possibilities for you to bless and serve others, whether you have experienced the loss of a child or not. Those of us, who have lost children, desperately *want* our little ones to be acknowledged. We *want* you to talk to us about them and to listen to us repeat our story to you, even if it is the 20th time. We *want* to hear their names spoken, remembered, and cherished by our family and friends. The most important thing to remember is that it was not just a "miscarriage" or a "stillbirth," it was the *death* of a much loved and very much desired child.

As I bring this book to a close, nearly two years after I began this journey, I would like to update you on our current circumstances. When Carter turned 10 months, my husband and I both agreed that we were ready for another child. We

195

did not, however, agree on *how* we wanted another child. Kevin was very set on having another biological child, and I desperately wanted to adopt, especially because of my ongoing health complications. It was time for a compromise. My father recently told me, "Sometimes compromise is not 50/50." After some discussion, we decided that we would try for another biological child, and leave the outcome to God, both agreeing that – given a healthy full-term pregnancy – this would probably be our last biological child. As much as it will definitely be a difficult decision, especially emotionally, we also agreed that I would most likely have my tubes tied following the birth of this next baby. My physical condition needed to be addressed. I could not continue with my current remedies forever. Lastly, as we both still feel that we would like more children in the future, we also agreed that adoption would be left on the table as a viable option.

In July, only a couple of months after we began working towards another pregnancy, I had a routine appointment with our family doctor, who felt that I should have my thyroid gland checked by a surgeon as soon as possible. He scheduled an ultrasound of my thyroid for that following week, and I scheduled the necessary appointment with the surgeon. Only days before my scheduled appointment with the surgeon, we discovered that I was already pregnant! We actually got the positive home-pregnancy test on the morning of our 11th wedding anniversary, August 12th. This would put our due date on April 15, 2012 – tax day!

We did not know if God would allow us to carry this baby to term, or how long He would allow us to "parent" this child, but we were resting in His promises. I was not afraid this time, as I had definitely grown in my assurance that His ways are *always* best. Like one small piece to a very large puzzle, my previous miscarriages were just a tiny part of what God has planned for the "masterpiece" of my life's story. I cannot see the whole picture right now, but I need to trust that He is placing the proper "pieces" in the proper places to create the finished image that He desires for my life – an image which mirrors the likeness of His Son.

Excitement was unquestionably my initial emotion, after those two tell-tale pink lines declared the existence of a new little life growing inside me. I quickly sent a picture of the positive test to two of my closest friends. One of them responded back to my announcement by asking me how I was *truly* feeling about being pregnant again, knowing the details of my situation. I thought for a brief moment and quickly text back, "God has spoken. Bring it on!" I knew it was not going to be easy, but I knew that my God would see me though, just as He always had in the past. I have found much comfort and reassurance in the following passage:

> ***Romans 8:15-18,26-32,35-39*** *- For ye have not received the spirit of bondage again to fear; but ye have received the Spirit of adoption, whereby we cry, Abba, Father. The Spirit itself beareth witness with our spirit, that we are the children of God: And if children, then heirs; heirs of God, and joint-heirs with Christ; if so be that we suffer with him, that we may be also glorified together. For I reckon that the sufferings of this present time are not worthy to be compared with the glory which shall be revealed in us.*

> *Likewise the Spirit also helpeth our infirmities: for we know not what we should pray for as we ought: but the Spirit itself maketh intercession for us with groanings which cannot be uttered. And he that searcheth the hearts knoweth what is the mind of the Spirit, because he maketh intercession for the saints according to the will of God. And we know that all things work together for good to them that love God, to them who are the called according to his purpose. For whom he did foreknow,*

he also did predestinate to be conformed to the image of his Son, that he might be the firstborn among many brethren. Moreover whom he did predestinate, them he also called: and whom he called, them he also justified: and whom he justified, them he also glorified. What shall we then say to these things? If God be for us, who can be against us? He that spared not his own Son, but delivered him up for us all, how shall he not with him also freely give us all things?

Who shall separate us from the love of Christ? shall tribulation, or distress, or persecution, or famine, or nakedness, or peril, or sword? As it is written, For thy sake we are killed all the day long; we are accounted as sheep for the slaughter. Nay, in all these things we are more than conquerors through him that loved us. For I am persuaded, that neither death, nor life, nor angels, nor principalities, nor powers, nor things present, nor things to come, Nor height, nor depth, nor any other creature, shall be able to separate us from the love of God, which is in Christ Jesus our Lord.

On September 28th, 2011, we went for our first ultrasound. I calculated that I was around 12 ½ weeks pregnant. As the technician placed the ultrasound wand on my stomach and began to push the cold gel around, a black and white image appeared on the screen and, immediately, my heart sank. I could make out a small form, but quickly saw the tell-tale signs of miscarriage – no movement and no heartbeat. It was quickly confirmed that our sweet baby #5 was now in the arms of Jesus. The doctor was not absolutely sure when the baby had passed. He/She appeared to be about the size of a 9 week old baby, with many characteristics of only a 6 week old baby. However, unlike the former miscarriage, we could see some of the bones within the little body, as well as the tiny little hands and feet. Despite the younger appearance of the fetus, Dr. Miller felt that it was possible that the baby had passed more recently, as my body had not begun to "break down" anything within my womb yet. Everything was in "perfect" condition. Obviously, this little one was only meant for heaven, right from his/her conception. Another baby created for God alone.

We decided to name this baby "Bliss Grace." "Bliss" means "perfect joy," and I can think of no greater way to describe how I feel about the amazing and endless grace of our loving Heavenly Father. Channing, who is now 3 ½, is taking the loss of his little sibling much harder than I would have thought. His initial response was, "God is naughty. He took baby Pizza Ice Cream from us!" ("Pizza Ice Cream" was the name he assigned this baby from day one, and I think it will always be the special way in which we refer to this special member of our family.) I think this is the first situation, in which, I truly feel that my son will only learn the truth by watching *us*. It is certainly a reality-check for us. We need to guard every word, every action, and even every facial expression that escapes us.

Monday, October 3rd, I went into the hospital for the scheduled D&C. I fully expected my heart to be heavy; however, God's perfect joy quickly filled my entire being that day. After I was wheeled into the pre-op room, the many people who would be attending my surgery came in to introduce themselves to me. The last person to come in was the attending nurse. She introduced herself as "Joy." I thought I had heard wrong and asked her to repeat herself. What were the chances? After she confirmed that her name was indeed "Joy," I briefly explained to her about my previous miscarriages and about the book that I was working on. I told her how I had decided to give this newest baby a name that meant "joy." Just then, Dr. Miller came in and we shared the story with her. She was amazed as well, and we all agreed that it was certainly a "God thing." Dr. Miller mentioned that she had begun reading my manuscript and that she was enjoying the Bible verses. I thanked her as she left the room to prepare for my surgery. Joy came over to wheel to me to the O.R. and she quickly asked, "So, Bible verses…what church do you attend?" We began talking some more, and I soon discovered that this special nurse had not only suffered a miscarriage recently as well, but that she was also a fellow Christian! My heart was overwhelmed by this point. It felt as though God Himself had come to be with me, throughout this difficult procedure. Joy and I were laughing and enjoying the sweet fellowship between two believers, during the short trip to the operating room. We had several other hospital employees stop to ask us what could possibly make us so happy, considering the current circumstances. Joy was quick to reply, "I guess it's easy to be happy, when you know that God is in control!" I could not have said it better. God bless this wonderful nurse, who helped to turn this trying situation into a joyous event of rejoicing in our great God!

Nehemiah 8:10c - The joy of the LORD is your strength.

We are not sure exactly where we are supposed to go from here. It will take wisdom and leading from God, but we know that whatever happens, we are covered by the mighty hand of our loving Lord and Saviour. No matter what we may face, He will always see us through. God has promised that this life will be full of trials, but He has also promised that it can be filled with joy and peace beyond anything we can imagine. As I look toward the future, all that I can say is, "Bring it on!"

Philippians 4:7 - And the peace of God, which passeth all understanding, shall keep your hearts and minds through Christ Jesus.

Psalm 30:5b - *Weeping may endure for a night, but joy cometh in the morning.*

Post Epilogue

"Why?" Answered

I had every intention of publishing my book after the Epilogue. I have tried to complete this book three times now, and God just keeps adding to it. I absolutely must give another up-date to my most recent miscarriage and then, thyroidectomy. As I had previously mentioned, I had seen a surgeon about surgery, due to an influx of problems related to my thyroid gland. We had to post-pone the necessary surgery because of my recent pregnancy. After my miscarriage, on November 3, 2011, I went ahead and had my thyroid gland removed via a four-inch incision in my lower neck. A week later, I went to an appointment to see my endocrinologist and discuss my blood-work, medication levels, and pathology results. I was completely caught off-guard when my doctor informed me that they had found two cancerous cysts amidst the many other benign ones – one was 1mm and the other was 1cm. About six months ago, I had had a second needle biopsy on the larger growths on my thyroid, but both tests came back negative for cancer. (The first biopsy was a couple of years ago.) Unbeknownst to us, the cancer was not growing in the "obvious" larger cysts, but rather in the smaller, seemingly insignificant, ones. Detecting this cancer would have been very difficult, and quite unlikely, at least for a rather long time. I had no intentions of asking for an unnecessary surgery, and though I knew that future surgery was likely, we had babies on the brain!

As I have mentioned many times throughout this book, it isn't often that we are able to see the reasons *why* God chooses to allow trials and heartache to enter into our lives. Usually, if we do see some positive results, it is years down the road. In this situation, I was able to see the "why" almost immediately. After becoming pregnant with Baby Bliss in July of this year, I quickly noticed that the symptoms related to my hypothyroidism skyrocketed. My throat began to swell, and I had trouble swallowing and even talking, at times. It seemed that the pregnancy hormones had triggered a reaction that is quite common, but usually, not so dramatic.

The unbalancing of my thyroid hormones was likely also the cause of the untimely end to my pregnancy. I never did question God. I did not feel the need. I knew that He would only do what was best for me, even when I cannot see how or understand why. After the cancer diagnosis, I *knew* why. The doctor said that if I had carried the baby to term, it could have easily become an emergency situation for me and for the baby. No one knows how fast this cancer would have grown, or how long it would have been before it was discovered. It would have been at least two years before another biopsy would be ordered. I believe with all my heart that my precious child saved my life. I cannot think of any other way that this destructive disease would have easily been found.

I also shudder to think of what could have happened, if I had decided to rebel against God's plan and had refused to submit to my husband's wishes for another biological child. Even though, in my heart, I was hurt and, honestly, even a little bitter that my husband seemed to be ignoring my needs and desires, I had surrendered to his request to try for another child. God has not only used this situation to remind me of His faithfulness and His wisdom to control each aspect of my life, but also to reprimand me for doubting His promises to bless us, when we obey Him and the authority He has set up in our lives, even when we do not fully agree with the processes laid out for us. I apologized to my husband for my attitude, and I look forward to moving forward with plans of "family expansion" in the near future. I share this, because I want you to understand that faith and trust in God is a process. No one has "arrived," nor will we, until we enter the presence of our Saviour in heaven one day.

The next step for me is a simple injection of radiation to kill off the remaining thyroid cells. The cancer can return at anytime as long as any part of my thyroid exists, so taking steps to eliminate or at least reduce that risk seems the best idea. Besides a required "vacation" away from my two little boys and our three small dogs – due to my radioactivity – there are no major side-effects or negative drawbacks to this option. I had cancer. I survived cancer. I never even knew that I had cancer until I was already cured - another amazing blessing from an awesome and loving Heavenly Father. One trial created a path through another. I stopped questioning God a couple of years ago, and I know that I will definitely never question Him in the future. His way is best. Trust this, and you will find rest for your soul.